Women
Embracing
Creativity

Women Embracing Creativity

Unleashing Your Inner Artist

By Christina Thompson

© 2009 Christina Thompson

Cover photo © Dmitry Sunagatov | Dreamstime.com

For more information about *Women Embracing Creativity*, please visit http://www.womenembracingcreativity.com

Printed in the United States of America

ISBN 1-442-11690-0

"It is not because things are difficult that we do not dare; it is because we do not dare that they are difficult."

-Seneca

Thanks!

A million thanks to the Creative Spirit, my most trusted friend.

Thanks to my husband Andrew,
who fills every day with beauty and laughter.

Thanks to Velvet the Summerglen Cat,
for warming my feet as I wrote this book.

Thanks to the wise women of the January 2009 session of *Women Embracing Creativity*, for the insights, websites, exciting Thursdays, and for supporting my efforts to publish this book!

Christina Cucurullo
Wendy Isbell
Jenny Snyder

Thanks to the Inside919 Trustees,
for generously sharing their ideas over many hot breakfasts.

Thanks to my parents John and Kathy Thompson,
for shaping my early creative journey.

Thanks to Grandmother Thompson,
who first showed me the possibility of a creative life.

Thanks to Professor George Broussard
for trombone-related encouragement

and

Thanks to Professor Dennis Eadus
for teaching me the fine art of "puking."

Contents

Welcome to Your Creative Journey!

Welcome to *Women Embracing Creativity - Unleashing Your Inner Artist!* I am sincerely glad you picked up this book; your reading it has the potential to be the beginning of a long and rewarding creative journey, as well as a richer and fuller life.

Artistry exists in every discipline and creativity lives within every human mind, but often society says this isn't so. Although creating is a basic human activity, negative myths tell us that only misfits are creative. Despite the fact that all people have creative capabilities, we are shamed into thinking only a select few of us are "talented" enough to use them. As much as we may want to think of ourselves as imaginative musicians, artistic scientists, or simply creative *people*, it can be difficult to embrace these titles and proclaim our creativity to the world. In this book, we'll set aside our misconceptions and discover the beautiful and empowering truth about creativity.

This book is designed to help you uncover your unique creative abilities and use them with confidence in your life. You need not be an artist to reap the benefits of this book; it's meant for any woman who wants to more fully understand the creative path. As you learn the lessons in this book, you'll build a foundation of safety around your creativity, break down the blocks that hold you back from your dreams, and begin to fill your supply of inspiration. You'll have opportunities to practice creativity, so that creating becomes a familiar, easy activity that you can do at home, at work, anywhere. This is a book of beginnings, a simple guide to help you take your first steps on the creative path with freedom and ease.

Although many of the experiences we'll discuss here are centered on artistic endeavors like music, writing, and visual art, this book can help women in any discipline uncover and develop their true creative talents. The arts are the common ground where we build connections with fellow creative people, strengthen our relationship with our Inner Artist, and celebrate our individuality. They're dynamic communicators with the power to reveal profound truths to a variety of people. When we engage in artistic play, we experience excitement, open-mindedness, and flow—all of which can help us express our creativity in any way we choose.

WHY THIS BOOK IS HERE

This book was originally developed as the workbook for a course by the same name that I teach at Summerglen Music in Raleigh, North Carolina. I designed the book to be a simple guide to help women unlock their true creative talents, and it's worked well! Women who tiptoe shyly into our first meeting grow empowered and gregarious within the span of a few weeks. We develop deep, lasting connections with fellow women who are walking the creative path, and perhaps more importantly, we have FUN playing with our newfound creativity. By publishing this book, I hope to extend the benefits of this course to an ever-widening circle of wise and creative women.

I wrote this book and developed the accompanying course simply because I was tired of witnessing strong and capable women telling themselves they had no talent. Hearing people falsely accuse themselves of tone deafness, inability to generate ideas, and absence of certain brain structures was getting terribly old, and I felt a call to do something about it. Something positive, empowering, myth-busting. This is my something.

This book is a collection of lessons I've learned along my creative journey. In these chapters, I share strategies that have helped me uncover, nourish, and use my creative talents, in hopes that they might help you as well. While the specialized techniques, theory, and history of artistic disciplines can be exceedingly complex, I've found that the basic workings of creativity are quite simple and accessible to all. By practicing the easy ideas found in this book, I have been able to tackle even the most advanced and challenging endeavors with a sense of confident serenity.

I was not the "talented" kid on the block, and throughout my musical studies I was somewhat of an underdog. Today, however, I enjoy a rewarding artistic career as a result of developing and practicing good creative habits. Although my chosen art form didn't come easily for me, I learned to "suit up and show up" at my trombone, no matter what. Whereas society harped on talent, I trained myself to focus on practice. When I encountered cruel myths and double-standards designed to discourage creative women, I calmed my mind by placing my trust in a protective Higher Power (The Creative Spirit) and my attention squarely on my creative intuition (The Inner Artist). Today I have the distinct satisfaction of having persevered through difficulties to build a blissful creative life, and the skills to continue on my journey. You can easily develop these skills, too, and enjoy a fruitful and rewarding creative journey of your own.

HOW TO USE THIS BOOK

This book is actually an eight-week course that you can complete alone or with friends. (If you're interested in becoming an official *Women Embracing Creativity* Guide and leading groups of your own, see page 159.) Throughout the course, you'll be asked to work on developing good creative habits, and each week, you'll need to read a chapter and complete your Creative Homework. Fully participating in this course will add several new responsibilities to your weekly schedule, so be prepared to set aside some time to give these activities a try. You'll find that this book works if you work it; the more effort you devote to incorporating these simple creative lessons into your life, the better your results will be! With that being said, also remember to be kind to yourself and cut yourself some slack. If you can't finish everything on this pass, keep in mind that this book is yours forever, so you can read it again and learn new things.

Also, I encourage you to *play* with the book. Play is at the heart of creativity, and the experimental nature of play brings you both a sense of giddy fun and a foray into beneficial higher-order thinking. If you get an idea while reading this book, go ahead and try it! If you see another way to do something I've presented, give it a shot! The act of taking what's in front of you and doing something different with it is *creating*, so I encourage you to check out the ideas in this book from many angles, play around with them, challenge them. And by all means, HAVE FUN!

Our book is divided into three sections. Because many of us have a tendency to place others' needs ahead of our own, the first three chapters will focus squarely on ourselves. In Chapter One, we'll examine our thoughts and beliefs surrounding creativity, discover their origins, and learn how they've been affecting our creative abilities. We'll meet the Inner Critic and the Inner Artist, and learn how to help them work together productively. Chapter Two finds us rediscovering who we are—our personalities, dreams, and desires—so that we can walk the creative path as our true and authentic selves. In Chapter Three, we gather tools to help us manage the ups and downs of making positive changes in our lives, giving us a foundation of safety as we move deeper into our creative journey.

Chapters Four and Five ask us to rethink our views on the world. Just watch the news, and it's easy to see how much uncertainty and negativity surround us each day. Here, however, we turn our attention to the positive aspects of life—abundance, freedom, and possibility. These middle chapters are the most spiritual of the course, strengthening us with gratitude and trust, and introducing to us a kind Creative Spirit who guides us along the creative path.

In our final three chapters we'll explore the creative process itself: how it unfolds, what we can expect, and how to maintain a creative life. Here we'll set aside popular myths and present a more accurate view of creative life and work. In these chapters, we're invited to develop and begin practicing our own understanding of living creatively.   My hope for you is that, through this course, you can develop a new perspective on your abilities and an empowering view of your creative talents that enables you to say, "Yes, I am a creative person!"

Some Things to Expect in This Course

In taking this course, you are beginning a journey to uncover and embrace your true creative talents. Learning to understand and use your creativity doesn't happen overnight; rather, your talents will be unveiled gradually through a process of nurturing and open-minded exploration.

Many of us begin this journey because we wish we were more creative, or because we have a sense that we're very creative, but don't know how to release our creative energy or realize our ideas. Some of us have artistic dreams that we've put on the shelf in favor of being "realistic," and now we don't know how to make those dreams come true. For some of us, these dreams are very specific: "I want to act, I want to make pottery, I want to play trumpet!" For others, it's a simple desire to live a more creative life, with more spontaneity, freshness, and depth.

As we embark on this creative quest, we undertake an emotional and spiritual journey. We may be super-excited at first; on the other hand, we may feel awkward and resist the changes trying to enter our lives. Anger or grief may rush forth as we recall ways our creativity has been stifled, and let go of what might have been. We may feel a strange mixture of anxiety, hesitation, and thrill as we blaze a new creative trail in our lives. Like the pioneer women traveling west, we're on a wild journey, both dreaming about our destination and missing the familiar things we left behind. We're balancing our regular activities with the new challenges of the trail. At times we may feel like we're on an emotional roller coaster—up and down, back and forth, and this is OK!

As we move further along the path, some of us may feel an impulse to quit and return to life as usual; after all, we're venturing into the unknown. If you feel this way, it's a sign to push onward! When you push through the most stubborn roadblocks on the creative path, you end up with the sweetest rewards—the faith, confidence, and skill to turn your creative dreams into reality.

Making the effort to uncover and nurture your creative talents isn't the same as just taking a class or reading a book. If you truly engage in working to uncover your creativity, you may find that your life changes. You may notice yourself re-evaluating your old priorities, jumping at opportunities that once would have frightened you, or being a little more selective about who you hang out with. Being nice to yourself and including your own feelings in decisions will become a little bit easier. Life itself might become a little easier, a bit more fun, and much more sacred and sweet. Although the process of embracing your creativity is sometimes tough, it's a rewarding challenge that can bring exciting results to your life. You have a golden opportunity to become an imaginative, confident person who's ready to create something amazing.

Taking this course will not make you a professional artist; it is simply a way to help you uncover and activate your true creative talents. However, once you're in touch with your creative abilities and have a positive attitude about using them, the door is opened for you to begin using your creativity in a variety of ways. It is possible that the dawning of your career as a professional writer or painter lies within this course—if you find this to be true, take a deep breath, find a fabulous teacher, and begin doing the work to become excellent at your subject of choice!

Creative Habits

People by nature are creatures of habit; little routines comfort us, whether they're watching cop shows every Tuesday night or sipping our coffee each morning. One easy way to invite more creativity into our lives is to cultivate habits that encourage us to use our creative talents. Throughout this book, we'll work on developing two healthy habits: the Journal Habit and Creative Time. As you incorporate these creative habits into your life, you'll find that your ideas flow more freely, your worries are fewer, and creating becomes easier to do!

Journal Habit

Our Journal Habit is exactly what it sounds like—we get into a regular habit of writing in a journal! Our Journal Habit is something we'll practice doing every day during our course, until it's as routine as brushing our teeth. Although cultivating a Journal Habit takes some effort, you'll find that writing regularly brings great rewards.

Those of us who have journaled before may find that the Journal Habit is a quite different endeavor. When we think of keeping a journal, we might imagine recording specific events or feelings. We'd likely try to stay on topic and write fairly legibly; after all, our grandkids might read it someday! We approach our Journal Habit with less structure, writing freely whatever comes to mind, changing topics at will, not worrying how our writing sounds, and tossing grammar, punctuation, and spelling to the wind. As my incredibly wise (yet very down-to-earth) English professor Mr. Eadus once said, we bypass our perfectionist urges and just "puke!"

Our Journal Habit teaches us how to show up and express ourselves fearlessly. We have nothing to fear because there's absolutely no wrong way to write in our journals. We can write early or late, sloppy or neat, with any kind of writing utensil that strikes our fancy. There's no certain way we must sound and no subject is off-limits. I like to sit at the kitchen table with my cat and write whatever comes to mind until I've filled the front and back of one page. Once I ended up with a detailed rant about the American educational system, and another time an erratically-punctuated stream of petty worries I'd be humiliated to show ANYONE. Both were fair game! The bottom line is, if we write, we're right!

WHY DO WE GET INTO A JOURNAL HABIT?

1. Suit Up and Show Up Training - Many of us are great at thinking and dreaming about potential creative endeavors, but find it hard to actually sit down and begin. When we train ourselves to show up and express ourselves in our journals day after day, we find that working on other creative activities feels easier, more natural.

2. Out with the Old, In with the New - We all have worries, "what ifs," and nagging thoughts swimming in our brains. Writing in our journals lets us get rid of all this rotten stuff so we can focus on other things. When we pour the contents of our minds onto paper, we make room for new stuff to come in—clear thoughts, fresh information, and bright ideas. Nothing is too weird, zany, morbid, or petty to write about; it's much better off sitting on the page than weighing on our minds!

3. Jumpstarting the Flow - When we're fully engaged in creating, we experience flow. When in a state of flow, we lose ourselves in doing our thing; we're fully present and deeply connected to our work. We can use our journals to practice jumping into this flow. Often, our writing will start off clunky and awkward, and we won't feel like writing very much. But if we push ourselves to keep writing, no matter what nonsense comes out of the pen, flow often follows. Just as showing up helps make starting our projects easier, keeping the pen moving helps us experience the ecstasy of flow.

4. Practicing Self-Expression - As women, we commonly refrain from expressing ourselves because we fear that what we have to say doesn't matter. Many of us were taught to second-guess our ideas, so we tend to keep them hidden. To be creative, however, we must be ourselves. The journal is a safe place to practice listening to our thoughts and candidly expressing our ideas. Many of us discover ourselves as we write, and over time self-expression becomes easier, both in our journals and in other areas of our lives.

Our Journal Habit cleanses our minds of worries and teaches us valuable lessons that we can apply to our creative projects. As time goes by, we may see dreams, plans, and schemes popping up in our journals. Characters, lyrics, and cool ideas may begin to flow from our pens, and we get to know ourselves better as we write about our lives. Above all, though, the act of sitting down and writing, no matter what, places a creative activity squarely into our everyday routine, and makes creating something we just...do.

Creative Time

Just as we make time for important activities like work, sleep, and meals, we also must make time to nurture our creativity. It's important to build some time into our day or week to focus on being creative and playful. During this course, we'll be asked to incorporate three types of Creative Time into our lives: Creative Moments, Personal Time, and Group Play.

CREATIVE MOMENTS

Creative moments are small, brief creative activities that we consciously add into our day. Rearranging the stuff on our desks, drawing on a napkin while waiting for our food at a restaurant, and indulging in a mid-afternoon daydreaming session can all be done in less than five minutes, but they are powerful creativity boosters simply because they shake up our routines. When we make a conscious effort to add some variety to our lives, we change the way we think—and changing our thinking fosters creative ideas.

If you'd like to bring Creative Moments into your life but are unsure where to start, it can be helpful to brainstorm a list of quick and easy creative activities, and set out to do a couple items on the list each week. As you make your list, think of fun and whimsical activities, silly little things you enjoy but never let yourself do. Here's a list of potential Creative Moments to get you started:

> **Listen to a new type of music.**
> **Strike up a conversation with someone new.**
> **Try a new restaurant or recipe.**
> **Pick a flower and press it in a book.**
> **Make a quick still life out of stuff in your house.**
> **Part your hair on the other side.**
> **Take a walk outdoors.**
> **Visit a random website and look around.**
> **Make up silly poems throughout the day.**
> **Enjoy a nice stretch and a big, deep breath.**

PERSONAL TIME

When we take Personal Time, we devote a block of time to nurturing our creativity on our own. One of the most pressing needs we have as creative people is time alone to think, decompress, and play around with our ideas. Even though we may not think we're very creative right now, it's important that we practice making time for creativity in our lives. We can begin by making a commitment to take an hour or so of Personal Time each week during our course. This encourages us to make creativity worthy of a spot on the calendar, and gives us quiet time to get to know ourselves better and do the creative exploring we want to do.

Although Personal Time involves only one person, ourselves, it also allows us to build relationships with our spiritual friends, the Inner Artist and the Creative Spirit. The Inner Artist is our childlike creative intuition that, when well cared for, bubbles over with exciting ideas and inspiration. During our Personal Time, we can nurture our bond with our Artist by indulging in activities she loves, like coloring, buying funky toys from the dollar store, or plunking around on the piano. To learn what our Inner Artist likes to do, all we have to do is invite her out to play. When she feels safe, she'll give us ideas, and we can strengthen our bond with her by trying them out. We can nourish our connection with our creative higher power, the Creative Spirit, by taking time to pray or meditate, practicing gratitude, and paying attention to the subtle details of our lives.

GROUP PLAY

As women, we tend to work very well in groups. Surrounding ourselves with understanding friends gives us a feeling of camaraderie, allows us a safe place to express ourselves, and encourages us to think about and build upon each others' ideas. When we find other women who are walking the creative path, it can be extremely fulfilling to hang out together and play. A group of creative women can devise bucketfuls of exciting ideas and plans that can make our creative journey even more rewarding. Playing with a supportive group can give us courage to try new things, share our ideas, and express our truest selves.

When you're planning Personal Time or Group Play, try thinking of some simple and fun things you've always wanted to do, but you've never seemed to have the time. These might be good things to do with your Inner Artist or your creative friends. Take that drive in the country you've been meaning to take. Watch that old movie you've always wanted to see. Check out that new Indian restaurant you keep thinking about. All of these can be great ways to fill your creative reserves with new experiences.

With any kind of Creative Time, we must make a commitment to do it and follow through. We put Creative Moments on our to-do lists and make sure we check them off by day's end. We schedule Personal Time in our planners and hold it as sacred as any business meeting. We resist the urge to blow off Group Play sessions with our friends. To our adult minds, taking time to create may seem unnecessary; however, once we let go of our reservations and try a bit of play, we find that Creative Time is vital to our creative well-being.

Some of us may feel threatened by the possibility of spending quality time with our creative selves. We may feel guilty for having neglected our Inner Artist in the past, and fear what might happen when we face her. Or, we may feel uncomfortable expressing our creativity around other people. Our minds may protest, "This Creative Time stuff is baloney! It's just going to waste my time and make me look stupid!" Worries like these are courtesy of our Inner Critic, who uses fear to separate us from our creativity. These fears may feel powerful, but each time we choose to set them aside and practice good habits, we bring ourselves closer to realizing our creative dreams.

Writing in our journals frees space in our minds, and Creative Time fills that space with new energy, understanding, and experiences. Each minute we spend imagining and playing fills our pockets with valuable creative capital. As we gather more and more creative resources and energy, we find it easier to act on those things we've always wanted to do.

Three Creative Habit Rules

1. Do it! The key word in Creative Habit is *Habit!* Many of us mistakenly think that creating is a rare event that happens only when we're touched by some far-off "muse." In reality, creating is a way of life that we can practice daily. Committing to regular writing and Creative Time teaches us to create, not procrastinate.

2. Be generous with yourself. Creativity flows, and to experience this flow, we must fully engage in what we're doing. When you journal, be sure to fill a couple of pages. When you're planning your Creative Time, be sure to set aside plenty of time so you don't feel rushed.

3. Keep your habits sacred. One goal of this course is to learn how to set healthy boundaries around our creativity, and this is the first one! Unfortunately, habits that are healthy for creative people may seem quite strange to others. Although we may be excited about our new habits, we must realize that sharing them with others may invite unnecessary criticism. Many of us feel that we need others' approval to know we're doing the right thing, but this is not the case when we're unleashing our creativity. Showing our journal entries to others, or telling not-so-understanding people about our latest Creative Moment can be harmful to our budding creativity.

On We Go!

On the next page, you'll take the first steps of your journey toward unleashing your creativity. As you continue through each chapter of this course, I encourage you to practice integrating these simple creative habits into your life. When practiced regularly, these habits can lay a foundation for a lifetime of enjoyable and flowing creativity. And now, let's get started!

> *The creative is the place where no one else has ever been. You have to leave the city of your comfort and go into the wilderness of your intuition. What you'll discover will be wonderful. What you'll discover is yourself.*
>
> *-Alan Alda*

Chapter 1
Making Room for Creativity

Goal: To uncover worries and fears we may have about creativity and begin the process of letting them go.

Artists-in-Hiding

We have all heard of Artists-in-Residence at colleges and festivals, but how about Artists-in-Hiding? Although the Artist-in-Hiding isn't a prestigious post you'd find at a university, it's a very common position for people to occupy. Many of us are Artists-in-Hiding, worried about what others will think if we create, whether we're "good enough" to create, or if people will laugh at what we do. Myths about starving artists, negative messages from the media about creative talent, and cautionary advice from well-meaning parents and teachers can scare us, whether we're young or well into adulthood, and can push our creativity into hiding. Here we'll explore some of the reasons that people fear being creative, and begin the work of dismantling our hiding places.

THE MYTH OF THE STARVING ARTIST

Let's face it; money is something we all need. We need to be able to provide for ourselves and for our families. We need food, clothing, and a safe place to live. Unfortunately, many of us have heard for as long as we can remember about the fate of the Starving Artist. Many of us were taught that being an artist, musician, dancer, DJ, or whatever for a living was a surefire path to bankruptcy and starvation. In the process of being fed this fallacy by well-meaning teachers, parents, and other figures in our lives, we became fearful of acting on our deepest desires, worried that if we dared to do something we loved, we'd pay an unbearable price.

As a youngster, I had a puzzling, yet all too common experience with the Starving Artist myth. Growing up, I heard adult after adult say, "You can do anything you set your mind to!" However, when as a high school senior I announced my plans to attend music school, nearly everyone who heard the news fretted, "Are you sure about this? Making it in music is hard!" or asked what my second major would be, because "Music doesn't pay the bills!" I went to music school anyway, because I am profoundly stubborn. But some of my art-school-bound friends who faced the same warnings got scared that they'd starve, put their paintbrushes down, changed majors, and now miss the creativity they left behind. MANY of us end up in this situation, because the thought of living in abject poverty is definitely not pleasant!

Even if we're not planning on quitting our jobs and becoming full-time artists, the Starving Artist myth can still be scary enough to make us limit our explorations of creativity. "I'd better not enjoy this painting thing TOO much. Painting can't pay the bills, so I'd better be sensible and only do it once in a while."

NEGATIVE INFLUENCES FROM MEDIA and CRITICS

Have you ever sat down and read a movie or theatre review in the paper, and been stung by the absolute meanness emanating from the critic's pen? Or, have you enjoyed a singer's performance on a television show only to hear a panel of judges trash the singer afterward with harsh put-downs? These situations make you want to run out and write a play or sing a song, don't they! Hardly. The world can be a rough place for creative souls, simply because criticism is a very easy thing to do.

In the December 2008 issue of *Psychology Today,* psychologist Judith Sills hits the nail on the head, saying, "In thirty years of practice, I've seen only one universal truth: No one needs to be coached to have negative thoughts." Negativity, unfortunately, comes very naturally to us human beings. It's no surprise that fear of having others' negativity turned on us—by being mocked or criticized for something we've created—is a powerful motivator for many people to remain Artists-in-Hiding.

Fear of criticism can also push us down the dangerous slope of perfectionism. When we get stuck in the cycle of trying to make our creations flawless, refusing to start working until we have the perfect plan, or not acting on our ideas because we're not sure they'll turn out perfectly, we get stuck doing one thing and one thing only—NOT creating!

Hearing harsh criticism and misleading messages about creativity in the media can also reinforce the misconception that only a select few have creative talents. This idea is false precisely because every one of us is designed to be creative. Even though we're not the fastest or strongest animals in the forest, human beings are at the top of the food chain simply because we have the ability to be creative. We can use our brains to solve problems, invent tools, devise plans, AND create works of art! Often, we fail to use our creative capabilities not because we don't have any, but because we're worried about falling short in our overly-competitive society.

PARENTS, TEACHERS, AND PEERS

To feel comfortable expressing our creativity, it's important to place ourselves in an environment where our ideas are supported and encouraged. This doesn't have to be difficult now that we're adults, because we can consciously choose to surround ourselves with creativity-friendly people. However, we didn't have that luxury when we were children. If our parents and teachers weren't creative types, they may not have put a high premium on nurturing the wild ideas and dreams we had as children.

Unfortunately, many of our parents and teachers were affected by myths about creative people, as well as society's sometimes negative notions about creative talent. Genuinely concerned about their children's future well-being, many parents will unwittingly stifle a child's artistic curiosity. When a child might need to hear, "Yeah, you should try acting; you might be really good at it!" they instead might receive a warning about what happens to people who make-believe instead of study. Likewise, teachers are under so much pressure to produce academic success, they may unconsciously marginalize kids' creative urges in favor of fulfilling state requirements: "If you don't learn your math facts, you'll fail the EOG test! So stop doodling in that notebook of yours and pay attention!"

Although among kindergarteners, artistic ability is all the rage, as kids grow older, the "coolness" factor of creativity begins to wane. Creating is a process, and learning the ins and outs of artistic endeavors takes a great deal of time and effort. Video games and television, on the other hand, provide much quicker gratification, and since the adults keep saying that creativity isn't very important anyway, many kids start thinking of the arts as "little kid" stuff that they want no part of. Many older kids truly enjoy creative and artistic activities, but don't want to tell their friends for fear of rejection. As the years go by, some kids stick to their creative pursuits, but many fall away and chalk it up to their having no talent. And they grow up to be Artists-in-Hiding.

HOW DOES IT FEEL TO BE AN ARTIST-IN-HIDING?

Faced with all these obstacles, many of us become too intimidated to jump into the pool of creativity and seriously explore our dreams and ideas. Some of us may stuff our creative dreams down so far that we barely realize we have them. Unaware of the true depth of our creativity, we become Artists-in-Hiding, insisting we have no talent but secretly wishing to create. Filled with self-doubt, we resign ourselves to sitting on the sidelines, watching other people enjoy the creative fun we long to experience.

If you're an Artist-in-Hiding, you may feel a discomfort in your life that is hard to put your finger on. You may feel like what you're doing now just doesn't fit, or find yourself wondering, "Is there something more?" You may feel an urge to paint, or write, or dance, or have a feeling that you can approach your work in a radically different way, but something always seems to hold you back.

You may find that you are your own worst critic, second-guessing your ideas and feeling like you're incapable of creating anything good or meaningful. This poor self-treatment sets us on a debilitating treadmill of doubt—the world around us discourages our creativity, and we respond by disqualifying our creative desires.

This endless cycle of self-doubting and self-judging leaves us even more afraid to step up and try something new, and keeps us stuck as Artists-in-Hiding.

COMING OUT OF HIDING

This world can be a harsh place for artists...and anyone, really. We begin our journey out of hiding and into the light of creativity by becoming willing to care for ourselves and to take our ideas seriously. Creativity flourishes in an atmosphere of nurturing and support; when we make the decision to start treating our ideas with respect, we set the wheels of creativity in motion. Instead of hiding, we can learn how to create a sanctuary for our creativity. When we value, nurture, and protect our creativity, we're likely to find that expressing our ideas becomes easier.

"Wow," you might be saying, "How do I go about protecting my creativity? And how can I respect my ideas if I don't really know if they're good or not?" The answer is simple: Practice! Starting today, practice taking good care of yourself. Practice dismantling your old hiding place by being willing to say, "That idea of mine might be pretty good!" Practice writing in your journal each day, and incorporating Creative Time into your week. With regular practice, you can learn to cherish your ideas and allow yourself to discover the joys of creative play. When you practice taking yourself and your desires seriously, you will begin to notice changes in your life—for the better!

As you begin this creative journey, keep in mind that it's not your fault if you haven't been able to achieve your creative dreams; you simply didn't have the information you needed to unleash your creative talents. Now that you know some of the causes of creative gridlock, you can practice taking small steps each day to nurture yourself toward greater creativity. One way to care for yourself is to learn more about how you operate, so we'll begin by exploring two personalities that reside in our minds and impact our creativity: The Inner Critic and the Inner Artist.

The Inner Critic and the Inner Artist

The human brain is a beautiful thing. It directs all our physical and mental functions, and is in constant contact with every cell in our bodies. It enables us to think, to feel, to decide, to speak, to sing. And since the dawn of humankind, the brain has helped us to survive and thrive in the world. One of the brain's built-in security measures is the ability to assess threats and keep us away from them. If our ancestors saw a strange new visitor near their village, this ability would kick in and say, "Unknown! Dangerous!" and make them ready to respond to potential danger.

As modern human beings, though, and especially as people on a creative quest, this survival tendency can sometimes hold us back. Creating things isn't usually mortally dangerous, but nevertheless a voice in our heads pipes up to warn us that we're in for it if we do this or that creative thing. I like to call this the Inner Critic. The Critic is on the lookout for new and strange things, ready to warn us that they're risky and keep us away from them. But the Critic doesn't limit itself to hungry predators. An abstract painting, a novel type of music, or an unfamiliar dance may register with the Inner Critic as nothing short of IMPENDING DOOM! The Inner Critic tries to control our actions with an endless supply of negative comments.

One important thing for us to understand is that when we decide to create something new, the Critic will respond by pelting us with everything it's got. The Critic does this not because it's mean, but because it's designed to protect us from potential dangers like criticism or rejection. It's our job to calm this impulse down, to realize it's there but not feed it with fear, and to nurture our Inner Artist to be confident enough to not take its comments personally.

Our Inner Artist is our creative intuition. She's the part of our brain that enjoys exploring, inventing, playing, and creating. It can be useful to think of our Inner Artist as a child, because she is very childlike: wide-eyed, energetic, and unabashedly honest. She likes playing make-believe, having fun, and trying new things. Our Inner

Artist thinks in a funky, eccentric way, and could care less what people think. On a hot summer day, when our Critic might say, "You'd better put on some sunscreen! You're going to get skin cancer, I just *know* it!" our Artist has a very different perspective, "Woohoo! It's so hot! Let's break out the sprinkler and PLAY!!"

Inner Critic can be compared to a worried parent, and Inner Artist is like a carefree child. When in balance, the Critic and the Artist can have a good relationship, with the Critic keeping the Artist grounded and the Artist keeping the Critic from getting too gloomy. Often, though, the two are out of balance, and the Critic ends up holding the Artist hostage by pounding her with negative, anxious warnings. One of our first steps in unleashing our creativity is liberating our Artist from the Critic's control.

Recognizing and Removing Negative Beliefs

On top of the Critic's warnings, we may have worries of our own about the creative journey. If we have never made a conscious effort to explore our creative side before, today we're venturing into unknown territory. What will happen if we're completely in touch with our creativity? What will our lives be like? Will everything change? When we step into the unknown, fear and worry often are there to greet us. One of the kindest things we can do for ourselves is to examine our worries and consciously decide whether we need them in our lives. Here are some common worries we may have about our own creative development:

> *People will think I'm self-centered for wanting a more creative life.*
> *Everyone will hate me/think I'm weird/gossip about me if I'm creative.*
> *I don't have any good ideas.*
> *What if my work stinks and people laugh at me?*
> *I might have to quit my job and change everything I know.*

More worries...

I might have to be depressed or self-destructive to create.

What if I run out of ideas? I'll look so stupid!

It's too late to begin now; I'll be so old when I get the hang of being creative!

I don't have the natural talent that other people have.

I'm too "normal" to be creative.

What if I have to move to a new city to do my creative projects?

Creativity is a luxury; I should just be happy with what I already have.

Although these are some fearsome worries, the good news is that they are just that: worries. Not facts. Not fate. Just worries! And not one of them need be true. Much of the time, our worries reflect popular myths about creativity more than they reflect the actual reality of living creatively.

Many of the worries listed above ask, "What if I'm not good enough?" Often, we stall out our creativity by focusing only on what we don't know. Since we're new to the creative path, we may feel uncertain about how to form ideas, start projects, or handle criticism. Many of us think that creative people just *know* this stuff, and if we don't just *know* it, too, we take it as a sign that we lack the "talent" to begin. In reality, many of us creative people don't know much at all at the outset of our endeavors! We begin, and then we learn along the way.

In addition to worrying about our own creative talents, we may harbor fears that reflect society's negative beliefs about creative people themselves. All too often, creative people are stereotyped as being moody, selfish, or weird by those who don't fully understand the creative process. Likewise, popular biographies about creative people tend to focus more on their eccentric ways or personal struggles than on the day-to-day reality of their lives. Ray Charles and Johnny Cash were both phenomenal musicians who made sweeping contributions to American music; however, movies about them focus more on their philandering ways, problems with drugs, and jail sentences than their musical masterpieces and creative processes. After years of hearing these negative stereotypes, we may worry that embracing our creativity will require us to transform into overdramatic, drug-addicted loners. On the other hand, those of us who don't feel like we fit into the stereotypical creative "mold" may become disheartened enough to quit before we even begin.

If we let them, our worries can push us away from our creative dreams and right back into our hiding places. Remember, not one of our fears needs to be true. We can be artistic, happy, sane, nice people. We can become more creative regardless of our personality, background, or age. We can live anywhere we like and enjoy a fruitful creative practice. A great way to overcome our worries is to build our confidence with positive, empowering beliefs. When we use the powerful tool of affirmations, we teach ourselves to think "Yes we can!" instead of "But something might go wrong."

POSITIVE AFFIRMATIONS

Affirmations are positive, empowering statements that we can use to break through our preconceived notions and turn negative beliefs on their heads. When we use affirmations, we do just the opposite of what the Critic and our worries do—we treat ourselves kindly and develop a sense of safety and possibility around our creativity.

Affirmations do just what they say they do—they affirm. They say yes to our creative desires, our true capabilities, and our Inner Artist herself. Unfortunately, many of us have trouble recalling the last time we said "yes" to our Inner Artist. Each time we've denied our creativity or half-joked that we have no talent, we have wounded our Artist. However, when we speak positively about our creative abilities, we acknowledge our Artist, uplift her, and help her heal. Affirmations are the first step in building a rewarding relationship with our Inner Artist.

When we first start working with affirmations, it may feel really weird to say nice things about ourselves. It can be tempting to say, "Man, this is cheesy; I don't want to do it!" Much of the time, this reaction happens because positive self-talk is very new to us. However, as we practice using affirmations each day, doing it becomes easier. Over time, our affirmations may stop sounding weird and start sounding *true!*

We don't need any special equipment or training to work with affirmations; we can create our own positive statements and use them anytime to build a sense of possibility around our creativity. One easy way to create affirmations is to think of some worries or stereotypes you may have about creativity, and practice saying or writing their exact opposite. "Creative people are flaky," becomes "Creative folks can be very conscientious and dependable." "I don't have any good ideas," is now "I am bursting with great ideas!" Using affirmations is an easy way to turn our minds into creativity-friendly places. Each time we turn a limiting belief into a positive, encouraging statement, we build a rich mental habitat where our creativity can flourish.

When we start working with affirmations, our Inner Critic is likely to freak out and start pounding us with negative objections. If we say, "I am an excellent musician," the Critic may yell out, "Everybody thinks you're a hack. You should just give up!" Objections like this may seem hurtful, but in reality, they can be powerful tools to build our creativity. Try this: every time the Critic pitches a nasty insult your way, choose to turn it around into a positive affirmation and throw it right back. Your Critic will absolutely hate that you're not listening, and start objecting with greater intensity. Eventually, though, the Critic wears itself out, and as you practice affirmations over time, it gradually becomes less and less aggressive. It's still there, but it's no longer dominating your mind and shooting down your ideas. When we show the Critic that it is no longer in control, we empower ourselves to begin achieving our creative dreams.

BOSS LADY - A FUN WAY TO SILENCE THE CRITIC

There are many ways to calm the Inner Critic, but I'll close this chapter with my favorite. When we step up and claim our title as the "Boss Lady" of our lives and minds, we empower ourselves to silence the Critic and begin working on achieving our wildest dreams. Best of all, this simple exercise can be done anytime, anywhere, in less than a minute.

Step 1 - Become the Boss. Imagine yourself sitting at a big mahogany desk in a prestigious office in your mind. This is your rightful place; *you* are the CEO of Your Life, Inc.! Imagine the perks of being a CEO: decision-making power, limitless resources, and the sheer bliss of being in charge. Allow yourself to imagine in great detail, enjoying the empowering feeling of being the boss. Feel free to come back to your "office" anytime you need to reclaim your distinguished executive title.

Step 2 - Fire the Critic. Visualize yourself, the boss, calling the Critic into your office. The Critic is a Safety Consultant who's run amok, generating so much red tape that your company can't get any work done. In any way that you see fit, thank the Critic for its services and send it packing. Watch the Critic walk out the door, and feel the sense of calm that descends over your life now that the Critic is gone. Remember, the Critic *can* be persistent; you may need to fire it more than once!

> *When I dare to be powerful, to use my strength in the service of my vision, then it becomes less and less important whether I am afraid.*
>
> *-Audre Lorde*

Creative Homework

1. Journal Habit - Remember to write a couple of pages in your journal each day this week. Do whatever you'd like to make your writing fun; buy a cool notebook, make yourself a nice cup of tea to sip as you write, or invite your pet to join you. And whatever you do, write!

2. Creative Time - It's time to start bringing some Creative Time into your life! This week, plan some Personal Creative Time and put it on your calendar. Now, think of some fun things to do with your time. Nothing's too wacky, as long as you can do it sometime this week. You may want to tell your family about this homework, and let them know you'll be busy at the time you've planned. Then, GO HAVE SOME CREATIVE FUN!!

3. Annoy the Critic! - Remember times in your childhood when other kids would say the opposite of everything you said to annoy you? This technique also works wonders with the Critic! This week, take every chance you can to write down the nasty things the Critic says to you, and then write their exact OPPOSITE several times. Your Critic will absolutely hate this, and after a while, it will back off in hopes that you'll leave it alone!

4. Sack O' Woe - Many of us hold negative beliefs about creative people or worries about what others will think of us if we're creative. From now on, if any of these come to mind, write them on a slip of paper and stick them in a paper bag. This is your Sack O' Woe, a place to store your worries so that you don't have to think about them. When you put a worry in the Sack, practice releasing it from your mind. Doing this is an awesome way to clear your mind today, and will be a great reality check later in our course!

5. The Critic's Hometown - Let's figure out where your Critic's mean comments come from. Using your list of nasty comments from #3, reflect on your past and determine where each comment might have originated. Which people and situations may have given ammunition to the Critic?

6. The Creativity Blocker Hall of Fame - When you do #5, you may recall some meanies who injured your creative self-esteem in years past. There's a place for these meanies—in the Creativity Blocker Hall of Fame! It doesn't matter if the Critic says you're being petty; if you think someone belongs there, they belong there. List your "Inductees" in your journal, along with a brief description of their crimes. Doing this work may pull up intense emotions as you re-feel the pain of being hurt or embarrassed. If so, keep writing, call your friends and vent, yell at the meanies on the page— whatever helps you cleanse these old hurts from your mind. This is an act of intense nurturing; you're standing up and protecting your Inner Artist AND yourself. You go, girl!

> **If you'd like to share your Creativity Blocker Hall of Fame story and read about others' Inductees, please visit:**
>
> **http://www.womenembracingcreativity.com/blockers.html**

7. The Champion List - This is the opposite of #6: List people who have supported your creativity and wished you well. Who are these people? What nice things did they say or do for you? How did you feel when you were in their company? Write down all the encouragement you can remember, and bask in its sunny glow.

7a. If you recall a particularly cool compliment you've received, try making it into a decorative sign and hang it somewhere you'll see it every day. Break out the crayons and have fun!

Chapter 2
Discovering You

Goal: To build a creative foundation by learning to nurture and understand ourselves.

Nurturing Our Selves, Our Relationships, Our Creativity

Many of us have an abundance of creative energy, but we find that we've given much of it away to help others realize their dreams. Just as we can easily spread ourselves too thinly in terms of time or physical energy, we can overextend our creative energies as well. We know that sleep can refresh our tired muscles, but what can rejuvenate our creativity? One of the easiest ways to nourish our creativity is to strengthen our relationship with ourselves.

Many endeavors require that we tailor ourselves to fit the demands of the world: as mothers we must support our kids, as drivers we must obey the rules of the road, as professionals we must dress for success. Creativity, however, demands the exact opposite: our real, raw, true selves. When we create something, we send a powerful expression of ourselves out into the world. We don't adapt ourselves to anything; rather, we allow our true selves to come out and play. Unfortunately, after many years of dressing to impress and fitting ourselves into various roles, it can be tough to remember who we really are. In order to create, we must reconnect to our true selves through patient nurturing and attention.

When we think of nurturing, we may imagine costly spa treatments and pricey weekend getaways that give us a break from the "daily grind." This definition of nurturing sounds quite selfish and frivolous, and implies that nurturing is only a once-in-a-while activity. Fortunately, nurturing ourselves is more than a superficial or occasional indulgence; it's an ongoing process that helps us build healthy relationships with ourselves and others.

Nurturing ourselves means that we become willing to view our own needs and desires as being worthy of attention. When we deprive ourselves of self-caring and consideration, we also deprive the people around us. When we give and give until we're empty, we're unable to be fully present for our loved ones. However, when we treat ourselves with kindness and understanding, we bring a happier, more secure version of ourselves into the lives of our families and friends. Consider the masks that drop when an airplane cabin depressurizes. The attendant always tells the adults to put their masks on first, and THEN help the children with theirs. When we put our masks on first by making sure to take care of ourselves, we in turn make it possible to be of service to others. We can begin to nurture ourselves by taking time to get to know ourselves.

What's True About You?

Knowing ourselves enables us to make conscious, informed choices about our lives, decisions that reflect who we are and what we want out of life. When we're not sure who we are, it can be easy to spend our lives "just getting by." Soon, the years pass and we find ourselves with dreams not realized and goals set aside. Often, creativity is one of these "shoulda, woulda, couldas." As we learn more about ourselves, we can better understand our dreams and design our lives so that we can accomplish them.

One of the biggest mistakes we can make in learning about ourselves is thinking that we can do it quickly. As with getting to know a friend, discovering ourselves is a lifelong process. We grow and change throughout our lifetimes and gain new experiences that shape our attitudes and thoughts. While it's unlikely we'll "find ourselves" simply by taking this course, we can use this opportunity to begin cultivating long-term habits that strengthen our self-understanding: listening to our intuition, paying attention to our feelings, and spending quality time with ourselves. When we invest time and attention into our relationship with ourselves, it will grow deeper and more rewarding over time.

Ironically, the other error we make in getting to know ourselves is thinking that we don't have time to do it. Many of us have so much going on each day that we can easily forget to check in with ourselves. Even though cultivating a connection with ourselves is a lifelong journey, we can take small actions every day to deepen our self-understanding. Here are several simple ways to learn more about yourself:

1. Spend some time alone each day. Turn off the TV, set aside your e-mail, and take a few minutes to just be. Allow your mind to wander and see where it goes. Or, take some time to reflect about things you love, goals you've accomplished, ideas you'd like to try—anything that comes to mind is fair game. Sometimes just sitting and thinking can help you uncover fresh insights about yourself.

2. Try a Creative Moment. If sitting and thinking feels awkward, Creative Moments can be great ways to spend quality time on your own. Doodle on a napkin, arrange things into a still life, play around on the piano, whatever. Don't worry about the quality of your art; just enjoy having a fun experience on your own.

3. Check-in throughout the day. Take a second here and there to observe your moods and feelings. How do you feel right now? What do you really want to do at this moment? When you keep in touch with yourself, you can gain valuable insights about your unique patterns of thoughts and feelings.

4. Take one (or several!) of those fun personality tests online. Sure, you won't get scientific results, but you'll have a good time, AND you'll learn a little about yourself as you answer the questions.

5. **Make note of the little things.** When you first start a romantic relationship, it's common to notice cute little habits that your new partner has: how he mashes his peas before eating them, how she twirls her hair when she's bored. Try noticing one little thing about yourself each day. How do you talk? What's unique about how you eat your food? Sit back and enjoy noticing your little quirks.

> *If one is estranged from oneself, then one is estranged from others too. If one is out of touch with oneself, then one cannot touch others.*
>
> *-Anne Morrow Lindbergh*

If these suggestions sound intimidating, or like ridiculous busy work that YOU surely don't need to do, this is a signal that you need to give them a try. Creative expression requires self-knowledge and authenticity—walking the creative path is extremely difficult if your inner self lies outside your comfort zone! Even the smallest efforts to learn about yourself can make a difference. Over time, these tiny actions can become a habit of self-discovery that helps you feel confident in yourself, clarifies your goals and desires, and invites the possibility of honest creative expression into your life.

The Importance of Being Nice to Yourself

As a music educator, I've seen firsthand the detrimental effects of negativity on music students' performance abilities. When a teacher acts like the Inner Critic, hulking over the student, nitpicking every note, and teaching from an angry, intolerant place, the student shuts down and any chance for her to play to her full potential is lost. The student visibly caves in, and the performance becomes timid, weak, and full of mistakes. On the other hand, a positive, inviting teacher can draw the beauty, confidence, and strength out of even the most inexperienced student. A similar phenomenon happens with the way we treat ourselves. When we beat ourselves up, we cannot reach our potential. But when we *build* ourselves up, there's no limit to the great things we can achieve.

As people on a creative journey, we must place a high priority on fostering a positive relationship with ourselves. It is from this self-nurturing that creative excellence is allowed to emerge. In our busy lives, it can be very easy to relegate our needs to the back burner: How often have we thought of something we'd like to do, but immediately shot it down because something "more important" needed to be done? How many times have we invented some reason to deny ourselves a well-deserved reward? We can no longer afford to practice this type of behavior; we must instead train ourselves to do and say kind things to ourselves. Creativity flourishes in caring, supportive environments, and that support must begin within us. Here are ten simple ways to begin building a stronger, more nurturing relationship with ourselves:

1. Spend some time paying attention to your thoughts each day.

2. Use at least one positive affirmation daily.

3. Set reasonable goals for yourself.

4. Allow yourself a treat or two each day.

5. Feed your body good, healthy food.

6. Allow yourself to go to sleep when you feel tired.

7. Every so often, remind yourself to breathe. And do it, deeply!

8. Write in your journal and enjoy some Creative Time.

9. Practice saying kind things about yourself and graciously accepting compliments from others.

10. Don't be afraid to say "no" to extra responsibilities.

Self-Doubt Checkpoint

Trusting our creativity is a brand new skill for many of us, and it can feel quite strange at first. We may sometimes feel insecure and uncertain about what we're doing, and other times feel like the wisest, most creative women on the planet. This disconcerting ebb and flow can leave us vulnerable to the Inner Critic's negative influence. When the Critic notices we're getting stronger, it will try to beef up its offense as well; often, these attacks surface as self-doubt. An attack of self-doubt might sound like, "Well, I like being creative, but what if I'm doing it all wrong and everybody knows it but me? I must look so dumb! Oh, I should just quit!" Bouts of self-doubt like these can be painful, and even worse, they can snowball into huge blocks that seem impossible to pass.

When under the influence of self-doubt, we can easily become the worst saboteurs of our own creative development. Our doubt-fueled destruction is seldom obvious; now that the Critic knows that its insults don't work as well, it will try to ambush us in more subtle ways. A prime example of this sneaky sabotage is when we find ourselves seeking approval from people whom we know don't support our creative explorations. If we're tempted to tell an unsupportive person about our latest Creative Moment or show them our wild, rambling journal entries, we must first stop and ask ourselves, "Will doing this strengthen my creativity, or harm it?" Usually, this temptation signals the Inner Critic in its most sinister form, manipulating us into asking others to dismiss our creativity. If we respond to our doubts by telling a less-than-understanding friend about how much fun we had with our Inner Artist last night, it's unlikely we'll find a supporter to boost our spirits; rather, we'll probably find someone to reinforce our doubts. The Critic will celebrate, and we'll suffer.

Later in our creative development, self-doubt and sabotage can surface in other ways. We might be close to finishing our first painting, and suddenly decide it's no good and stop working on it. We may in a fit of self-doubt delete an excellent draft of our book, or tear up our latest song before we get a chance to play it through. Self-doubt can be a powerful enemy to creative people, but self-care is a potent antidote. Take care of yourself. Trust yourself. And by all means, keep going!

Another form that doubt often takes is our own skepticism about whether what we're doing will truly help us grow creatively. Throughout our lives, we've seen so many "miracle" products and heard so many farfetched claims, that it can be difficult to believe that anything can truly help us. To some of us, the idea that we have an Inner Artist and an Inner Critic battling inside our heads is too much mumbo-jumbo to accept. Others of us may strongly doubt that all people can be creative. When we set off in search of a new, fuller way of life, it's perfectly natural to have doubts like these. Sometimes skepticism protects us—it's probably steered us away from taking part in harmful get-rich-quick schemes and buying gadgets that don't work. However, when we're uncovering our creativity, skepticism and doubt can hinder our growth. It's times like these when we must identify our doubts, consciously set them aside, and practice open-mindedness. When we open our minds to examining our beliefs and trying new things, we allow the possibility of new and exciting experiences to enter our lives.

Dealing with Other People

So far in this chapter, we've learned about the importance of understanding ourselves and pushing past feelings of doubt. While cultivating a positive relationship with ourselves can go a long way toward strengthening our creativity, building healthy relationships with others can give us the support we need to sustain a robust and enduring creative practice. When we surround ourselves with people who nurture and encourage our creativity, we give our talents a place to grow! Here, we'll discuss ways to foster healthy, creativity-affirming relationships with the people around us.

NAYSAYERS AND NEEDIES

When we begin to make positive changes in our lives, some people around us may become uncomfortable. Perhaps these folks are stuck, and our success bothers them. Or, they may worry we'll no longer want them around once we've learned to use our creative talents. It's quite possible that these people themselves are Artists-in-Hiding, and watching us enjoy our creativity brings up the unsettling possibility that they can do the same: "If she found her creativity, maybe I can, too. Now I have no excuse to be hiding!"

For some, the possibility of change is so fearsome that they will sabotage us to make that possibility go away. A terse comment here, a well-placed doubt there, or a suggestion that we've "changed" are all ways these Naysayers can sabotage us. For people like us who are learning to tame the Inner Critic, such negativity can be detrimental. The Critic will grab any shred of doubt it can find and throw it at us hard: "Look! Your FRIENDS think you're crazy and selfish. Ha, I was right all along! So QUIT already!"

We may also encounter sabotage in the guise of neediness. We tell our families and friends that we're going to start writing in our journal first thing in the morning, and suddenly someone starts needing a ride every day at 6am. We let everyone know we're going on a cool creative field trip on Saturday afternoon, but oops, someone else has something "more important" they need us to do instead. It can be easy to fall into the trap of pushing our plans aside to fit the whims of others; after all, we're being nice, right? No. Putting ourselves last is telling ourselves that we're second-class citizens. And that, my friends, is not nice!

When we encounter people who try to criticize or sabotage us, we have a choice. We can either take their criticism personally and give up, or choose to take positive action. Here are some positive actions we can take when faced with Naysayers or Needies:

1. Stay on your side of the street. One easy way to safeguard our creative development is to keep Naysayers' views where they belong—on their side of the street. Often, when someone sends negativity our way, the problem is really about *them*. When we internalize others' negativity, it's like going across the street and taking out our neighbor's trash for them. When we leave other people's trash where it belongs, we have more energy to keep our side of the street (and our minds) clean and serene.

2. Be a teacher. Instead of growing resentful when people don't react the way we'd like them to, we can teach them about what we're doing and how we'd like to be treated. If your kids won't give you time to create by yourself, teach them how everyone, even mommy, has goals and dreams that they need to accomplish, and that these require time. Your "lesson" may even encourage them to follow a dream of their own!

3. Set boundaries. When we set boundaries and stick to them, we often find that people are more respectful of our time and efforts. One easy way to begin setting boundaries is to adopt a Purple Velvet Rope Policy.

THE PURPLE VELVET ROPE POLICY

In his bestselling business work *Book Yourself Solid*, Michael Port advises businesspeople to implement a Red Velvet Rope Policy to screen potential clients. The Red Velvet Rope is a standard that differentiates ideal clients from not-so-ideal clients. When a businessperson meets a potential client who respects and resonates with the business's values, she opens the Red Velvet Rope, allowing the client to reap the benefits of a fruitful relationship with the business. Those who aren't a good fit simply aren't invited past the rope. When businesspeople decide to work only with clients who have the qualities necessary to be allowed behind the rope, they make doing business much more fun; after all, they get to spend their time working with people whom they like and respect!

As people on a creative journey, we can adapt Mr. Port's business advice into a powerful tool for protecting our creativity. Just as businesspeople close their Red Velvet Rope to not-so-ideal clients, we creative people can close our own rope, a PURPLE one, perhaps, to people who don't support our creativity. Our Purple Velvet Rope places a protective shield around our creative ideas and desires. We can choose to open the rope to supportive and kind people, and close it to those who threaten the safety of our creativity.

A big part of respecting ourselves is learning to set boundaries in our lives, and the Purple Velvet Rope is just that. The rope is a boundary that protects our true selves: our real thoughts and feelings, our deepest desires, our wildest dreams, and our Inner Artist herself. The area behind our rope is like the vault in a bank, and the area outside the rope is the lobby. Anybody can walk into the bank, but not just anyone can go inside the vault. Just as inviting a thief into the bank vault can mean financial ruin, allowing the wrong person behind our Purple Velvet Rope can spell disaster for our creativity. Opening the rope to people who dismiss our feelings, second-guess our dreams, and criticize our desires can send us right back into hiding, stalling out our creative projects for years to come.

We can create our own Purple Velvet Rope Policy wherein we decide whom we'll allow to share in our creative endeavors and whom we'll keep at a distance. My policy is to keep overly negative people from my inner circle. I'll treat them nicely, but I won't dare trust them with my deepest feelings. My policy also has an educational component: if you express genuine interest in what I do, I'll teach you about it, and teaching is really a slow and measured opening of the rope. Having this policy has kept my Inner Artist well-protected, and has allowed me to have a variety of healthy relationships, in both the lobby and the vault.

One important thing to remember is that we don't need to feel guilty for choosing the people with whom we share our lives. As young girls, many of us were taught to "be nice," even if that meant allowing less-than-ideal people to monopolize our time and energy. I call this Nasty Niceness. Nasty Niceness is the twisted ideal that makes us hesitate to hang up on annoying telemarketers and shames us into spending time with folks we don't like. It bullies us not with fists or threats, but by exploiting our sense of kindness. When we're Nastily Nice, we're kind to others but cruel to ourselves. As creative people, we can no longer afford to practice this double-standard. Instead, we can gradually learn to replace Nasty Niceness with true kindness by using affirmations. If we feel guilty for setting boundaries, we can choose to change our guilt into an affirmation: "When I choose not to hang out with people who are negative, I am being kind to my Inner Artist and myself!" Just as affirmations can silence the Inner Critic, they can also help us become more comfortable with making positive choices in our lives.

TRUE FRIENDS

Our culture is one that celebrates independence, so many of us were raised to view self-sufficiency as the ideal. Even if we feel like we need help, we may hesitate to reach out to people because we fear they might be busy or think we're being intrusive. However, sometimes the thing we need most is the comfort of a good friend.

Today, we are healing from the creative wounds of our past. Our creativity was a broken limb for many years, and now we're putting a cast on it and allowing it to become functional again. But just as it would be difficult to put a cast on our own arm, it can be hard to pull off a creative recovery alone. We need to teach ourselves to reach out to others on the creative path and enjoy their company. When we share experiences, feelings, and laughs with a friend, our creative healing process accelerates.

True friends are those who celebrate our creativity, the people we're comfortable inviting past the Purple Velvet Rope. As we continue our creative journey, it will be helpful to seek out the true friends in our lives and practice reaching out to them. We can begin to build a circle of support by simply picking up the phone and taking a minute to talk with a friend. When we make time for friends, just like we make time for our Inner Artist, we allow ourselves the opportunity to build strong, healthy relationships that enrich both our creativity and our lives in general.

YOU, THE AMBASSADOR OF CREATIVITY

As a person on a creative quest, you may know more about creativity than anyone else in your circle. If you find yourself surrounded by people who don't understand what you're doing, rather than get annoyed, try turning the situation into a teachable moment. You are an ambassador for creativity, an educator. Try sharing your creative experience with others, even if you feel like you know only a little bit. You may be the person who clears up others' misconceptions about creativity, the walking example that it's possible to be a kind, responsible, financially sound creative person. Educating others about creativity also strengthens your own understanding of the creative process, and can make you feel great about what you're doing! Best of all, your input may be the spark that shows other Artists-in-Hiding that they too can come out and create.

Creative Homework

1. The Who You Are Exercise - Sometimes, society's expectations pile upon us over the years, and without even knowing it, we can forget the very essence of who we are. Fortunately, all it takes is a little time and reflection to begin to uncover our true selves, and we'll start by answering some simple questions. As you answer, write what first comes to mind, and don't edit yourself for fear of what other people might think. Write, reflect, and enjoy spending some time with yourself.

When I was a kid,
I was...
My favorite toys were...
My favorite things to do were...
I wished...
My strong qualities were...
I had a funny habit of...
I wanted to be a/ an___when I grew up.
I thought being an adult would be...

Today,
I enjoy...
If I had time I would...
One of my guilty pleasures is...
I am good at...
The best part about being an adult is...
I would describe myself as...
My favorite things to do are...
On a perfect day, I would...

In 20 years,
I will be...
I'd like to be able to say...
I will be good at...
My favorite thing to do will be...
My friends will say I'm...
On a normal day, I'll be...

2. List some ways to nurture yourself. - Pick one or two of these and practice them in your life this week.

3. Design your own Purple Velvet Rope Policy - What are some qualities that could get someone inside your Purple Velvet Rope? Which traits will keep them out? Will you offer an educational program to help people develop the traits that will get them inside? You decide. Write your policy down, and look for opportunities to practice it this week.

4. The "This is So Stupid" Exercise - Facing our doubts head-on can help us push through them and try new things in our lives. Here, we'll air them. Take a moment and write down anything that you've learned in our course so far that sounds like a heap of baloney. What are your doubts about becoming more creative? Write them down as you think of them. ALL of them!

5. Putting Aside Skepticism and Doubts - Using your list of doubts from #4, take some time to imagine the thing you doubt actually being true. If you doubt that you have an Inner Artist, write "What would happen if I DID have an Inner Artist?" Then, answer your question, and don't hold back. Imagine all the wonderful things that could happen if it weren't "too good to be true." After you've written a positive response to each doubt, pick some doubts and consciously try to set them aside (or turn them into positives) this week.

6. Self-Talk Day – One day this week, honestly listen to everything your mind says to you, and everything you say aloud about yourself. Write these down if you can. At the end of the day, think back over the things you heard your mind and yourself saying. Were they words of encouragement, confidence, and power, or were they words that made you sound weak and unable? It can be eye-opening to hear the things we say about ourselves. If you find your self-talk is negative, make a conscious effort this week to add more kind words to your repertoire.

7. Good Habits Checkpoint - Reflect on the creative habits you practiced this week. How is your life different as a result of using these new creative habits?

Chapter 3
Dealing with Growth and Change

Goal: To learn strategies to make ourselves comfortable even as we push outside our comfort zones.

As we unleash our creativity, we may find that our lives change. We try new things, feel different feelings, and begin to relate to the world in novel ways. Although we may not feel many growing pains at this point on our creative journey, it's important that we learn how to deal with issues that arise when we make sweeping changes in our lives. Changes, even positive ones, can pull us off balance and leave us feeling uncomfortable and awkward. Here, we'll discover tools to help us navigate the new territory of our creative lives. We can return to these tools again and again for support along the creative path.

On Growth

When we make life changes like unleashing our creativity, we push the boundaries of our comfort zones further and further outward. So far on our journey, we've had to experiment with open-mindedness, try new ideas, and incorporate new activities into our lives. Just as our muscles would ache after doing heavy physical labor, our minds and spirits can grow somewhat tender after weeks of mental and spiritual heavy lifting. We may feel odd, emotional, and not quite like ourselves; on the other hand, we may get the sense that we're more ourselves than we've *ever* been.

Growth is rarely a neat and tidy process. We may have a breakthrough one day only to feel like we've stalled out the next, and that's OK. Just as we were awkward as we grew from girls into teenagers, we're a little clumsy now as we grow to embrace our creativity. Our adult minds may dislike this unsteadiness; we may want to know what's happening and why we're feeling the way we are. We may feel frustrated when we can't produce tangible evidence of our creative development. This is a time to practice patience and just keep walking the path. When we were thirteen years old, we may not have felt many changes at all, or we may have noticed so many things changing it drove us nuts; either way, we were moving closer toward womanhood with each passing day. The same is true for creativity. Whether we feel like we're going nowhere or going crazy, we're inching closer to creative fulfillment. Just take it easy, do your creative work, keep being nice to yourself, and enjoy the journey.

One way we can deal with creative growing pains is to treat our growth as an adventure, and try to notice and savor every feeling, even the ones that don't feel so great. Even emotions that feel rotten, like fear, anger, and uncertainty can help us break through our former limitations and allow greater creativity to enter our lives.

Four Funky Feelings and How to Use them Wisely

As we seek a broader, more fulfilling life, we open ourselves to a string of emotions. We may feel emotionally raw from trying new things and pushing past our previous boundaries. Rethinking our beliefs and unearthing our old creative dreams can be highly emotional endeavors as well. Bouncing among the excitement, anger, fear, and uncertainty that accompany change can be difficult! Here, we'll explore several emotions that change often evokes, and learn how to use them to help us on our journey.

UNCERTAINTY

When we make changes in our lives, it's common to find ourselves in a strange no-woman's-land where we're no longer our old selves but not quite our new selves, either. When we have one foot in the old and the other in the new, it's natural to feel lopsided. When we feel unstable, it can be tempting to let ourselves fall back into the old—back to our familiar excuses for avoiding creativity, back to society's myths about talent, and away from our newfound awareness. Even though feeling off-balance isn't fun, we can learn something from feeling uncomfortable in our own skin. It's possible to use times of uncertainty to push even further past our limits and begin trying the things we've always wanted to do.

Sometimes we actually pay to feel uncertainty; a prime example is when we ride roller coasters. Roller coasters are designed to make us feel the exhilaration of uncertainty—just when we think we're going one way, there's a sudden drop, or we find ourselves careening upside-down through some crazy loop. Roller coasters are enjoyable simply because they make us move in unexpected ways, but we can enjoy the ride only if we embrace this uncertainty and turn it into excitement.

Uncovering our creativity is much like riding a roller coaster; in both, the only sure thing is change. If we accept that we're in for some twists and turns, we can embrace that inevitable unsteady feeling in our lives just as we'd embrace the roller coaster's wild ride. When we allow ourselves to enjoy the ride, uncertainty can be the spark that propels us to open our minds and try new things. Our Inner Artist loves the uncertain, so if we need help embracing the joys of feeling off-kilter, she's the one to see. "You feel weird anyway, so why not try salsa dancing?!" she may say. When we give her ideas a shot, our uncertainty often gives way to the excitement of discovery and the joy of new experiences.

FEAR

Fear can be a useful tool for keeping ourselves alive, but it can also hold us back from doing the exhilarating creative things we want to do. Fear is often a signal that we're facing something unfamiliar and uncomfortable. When living beings feel fear, we are faced with an ancient, primal choice: fight or flight. Are we going to run screaming back to our hiding places, or are we going to view that fear as a challenge that we're willing to take on? When we make a decision to face our fears, we empower ourselves to transcend our limits and discover new possibilities in our lives.

If we want to grow in our creativity, we must face the challenges that cross our creative path, even the ones we don't think we can overcome. Like Eleanor Roosevelt said, "You must do the things you think you cannot do." Since embarking on this course, we may have already faced—and beaten—several very intimidating fears. Overcoming the Inner Critic may have seemed impossible at first, until we learned how to respond to its attacks in healthy ways.

Letting go of our fears about creativity may have been difficult initially, but by examining them honestly and openly, we freed ourselves to enjoy our creative journey. In both of these scenarios, we faced a fear and stared it down, and now it doesn't seem so scary after all. When we feel fear, we must realize we have a choice. We can allow our fear to control us, or we can choose to look it in the face and take action!

Velvet, our cat here at Summerglen Music, is a perfect example of facing fear. He's a very territorial fellow who dislikes other cats' intruding on his "property," but he's declawed and has lost most of his teeth. Despite his lack of defenses, Velvet faces his adversaries head-on. When another cat approaches, Velvet boldly runs up to the cat, puffs up his fur, stares right into the cat's eyes and lets out an angry howl and hiss! Velvet's lack of claws has never been a problem for him, because he's never needed to raise a paw in defense. At the sight of Attack Velvet, most cats turn tail and run far down the street without looking back. The lesson we can learn from Velvet is this: even if we don't think we have the tools to fight our fears, simply facing them can make them run from our lives.

> *You gain strength, courage, and confidence by every experience in which you really stop to look fear in the face. You must do the things you think you cannot do.*
>
> -Eleanor Roosevelt

ANGER

With change often comes anger. Anger doesn't always feel good, but it can be a great friend for people who are making changes in their lives. Why? Anger is a huge motivator, a call for change. When we're angry, we want to DO something. We want to yell, scream, throw stuff. As creative people, we can harness the energy of anger to create positive change, to spark new ideas, and to begin working toward those goals and dreams we've always wanted to accomplish.

Most of us have been taught not to express our anger. We want people to think we're nice, so we hide angry feelings; we stuff them down and pretend we're "OK." When we hide anger in an effort to be acceptable to others, we stifle energy that can be vital to our creativity. Instead of breaking stuff, or burying our anger and having it grow rotten in our minds, we can try a third alternative— learning to channel and use our anger productively.

Anger is an urgent voice that demands to be heard. When we feel anger, there is usually a reason, a message that the feeling is trying to relay to us. If we take the time to discern why we're angry, we can learn exactly which actions we need to take. If we grow enraged at our family members for repeatedly intruding on our Creative Time, our anger may be telling us that we need to set boundaries and demand that people respect our time. If we're so frustrated at the dearth of good music on the radio that we want to scream, that anger may be prodding us, "Get started on that new song you've been wanting to write! Do it now!" Even though anger isn't the kindest or gentlest feeling, it can be a true ally on our creative journey. When we listen to it and channel it, anger can propel us into exciting new opportunities.

GUILT

Throughout our lives, we've been pelted with negative myths about creativity. We've heard that the arts are fluff, the packing peanuts stuffed around the "more important" things in life. We've been told that creativity is frivolous, and that pursuing things that truly interest us smacks of uncaring self-indulgence: "The economy is tanking and people are losing their jobs and our country is at war and you're PAINTING?!" These nasty negatives make us feel guilty for doing what we love and ashamed for being who we are. Guilt trips are toxic—to our creativity, to our self worth, to our souls.

On personal journeys of any kind, it's common to encounter guilt-tripping friends or family members. When others try to send us on guilt trips, it's often a sign that they're uncomfortable with themselves. They may fear that our changing will create pressure for them to change as well, or worry that we'll no longer need them if we follow our dreams. The guilt trip is merely a way to make us stop what we're doing so that *they* can feel secure again! An example of a guilt trip might be: you tell a friend how much you're enjoying your new creative activities, and the friend sarcastically retorts, "Wow, it must be *so* great to be creative. You must be *really* special. *Normal* folks like me just don't have the talent." Guilt-inducing comments like this can really sting, but the good news is we can choose whether to accept them or not. Guilt trips live in that garbage bag on the other side of the street, and we can decide to leave them there. We can even embrace guilt trips as teachable moments: "Of course you have talent, my guilt-tripping friend. Creativity is humankind's greatest strength!"

Sometimes, it's not others doing the guilt-tripping; it's us! When we're uncertain about the future and anxious about how our newfound creativity will affect our lives, we often try to guilt ourselves out of following our dreams. Fortunately, we've already learned everything we need to know to send guilt packing. When we find ourselves buying into myths that creating is selfish and unimportant, we can make a choice to turn these false messages into affirming truths. "I love to draw, but there are more important things I should be doing," becomes "Drawing is important to me; therefore, it's important enough to deserve my time." Above all, we must remember that creating is not a guilty pleasure; it's our birthright as human beings. When we create, we are not being subversive, egotistical, or uncaring people; we are simply being *people.* People create, and people are born to reach their potential. We are doing both, and for that we have no need to feel guilty.

Beginning Self-Discipline

On the outside, many creative people may seem a little scattered, a tad nutty, a touch disorganized. On the inside of every successful creative person, though, is a well-developed sense of self-discipline. We have to suit up and show up to create. We need to learn to listen for guidance and make sure that our creative work gets done. A great time to begin developing self-discipline is when we feel lopsided and funky, because the extra structure can help steady our feet and give us our bearings. In this section, we'll discover four easy ways that we can start stabilizing ourselves with self-discipline.

> *I know the price of success: dedication, hard work, and an unremitting devotion to the things you want to see happen.*
>
> *-Frank Lloyd Wright*

PERSEVERANCE

The key to sustaining a creative life is to regularly do creative things. We build a rewarding creative practice by showing up at our art form each day and taking regular time to nurture our talents. Many people think that artists just sit down and create masterpiece after masterpiece. No. We sketch and paint and practice each day, and the masterpieces come in time. When we make a commitment to creating regularly, being creative becomes an easier, more natural activity. We have been brushing our teeth daily (hopefully) since childhood, and we now do it masterfully, with ease and fluency. Believe it or not, creativity works the same way. Want to be a great songwriter? Start writing a song every day. Want to knit beautifully? Then knit regularly.

Perseverance means we persist in our efforts, even in the face of distraction or discouragement. Life provides many obstacles to distract us from creating, from traffic jams to others' agendas to our own procrastination. When we make creativity a steady presence in our lives, despite all the distractions we face, we are rewarded with stronger abilities, more confidence in our creative talents, and a stronger bond with our Inner Artist.

Perseverance is all about showing up and doing, not about the end product. Some days we'll wake up, write a horrendous song that borders on being embarrassing, and that's what we'll get for the day. This is just fine, simply because we showed up and did our thing. Doing our thing badly is much better than waiting until we're perfect to take action. We become better and better by doing and doing. When we set aside perfectionism and approach our art form as a chance to play, have fun, and grow, it can be easier to regularly engage in creative pursuits.

Just as we may have a morning routine of showering and getting dressed, we can establish a simple routine that gets us into a regular habit of creating. A creative routine can be as simple as improvising at the piano every morning at nine o'clock, or taking five minutes to draw before bedtime. Writing in a journal and taking Creative Time are creative routines as well. We can design our routine to fit our energy levels, our personalities, and our schedules. Whatever we choose to do, the key is regularity. When we create often, persevering past hurdles that try to stop us, creating becomes natural, flowing, easy.

LIVING IN THE NOW

As Artists-in-Hiding, we may be tempted to live out our creative dreams in our imaginations rather than doing the work to turn them into reality. Rather than living or working in the present, we spin our wheels by indulging in "shoulda, woulda, coulda" thinking. To be successful creative people, however, we need to learn to be present in each moment, and teach ourselves to notice what's happening around us right here and right now.

Sometimes we find ourselves worrying too much about the future or harping too long on the past. Both of these can be very time-consuming activities, but not very productive ones! Trying to imagine the outcomes of our creative projects, the reviews they will get, and other people's reactions to our work can cause us to forget the most important thing of all—to begin! Hanging on to past regrets and resentments keeps us from creating as well; after all, how can we fit into an art studio with all kinds of baggage tied around our waists? Baggage from the past and anxiety about the future are creativity snuffers; we can spend so much time managing them that there's no time left to do our creative work. When we live in the now, on the other hand, our minds and senses are less distracted. We can focus on our creative projects and work with freedom and intention.

Living in the now also means being present for each moment, knowing what's going on, and making conscious decisions instead of just going with the flow. Many of us lead distracted lives; we have so many things to keep track of that we end up keeping track of nothing. In our harried society, it can be easy to drive from obligation to obligation on auto-pilot, never stopping to see what the scenery looks like, or to ask that fateful question, "What am I doing here, anyway?" We cannot create on auto-pilot, and we can't innovate on cruise control. We must learn to pay attention.

PAYING ATTENTION

Many people think that the creative life involves a great deal of lazy, hazy daydreaming. In reality, creative people gather ideas and make them happen by noticing in great detail what's going on around us. How can a poet craft a beautiful line about glistening dewdrops playing among velvety red rose petals if she doesn't take the time to notice the rich texture of the petals, the sunlight on the dew, and the quiet serenity of morning? She can't! She must take the time to notice and appreciate the tiniest details of her day, and then she can use those details to create spectacular works of art.

If we're used to living fast-paced, on-the-go lifestyles, paying attention can feel like an enormous change. Living hurried lives, we feel constant pressure to go, do, and accomplish. Multitasking is the norm, even though our brains aren't designed to juggle a multitude of tasks at once. Being creative, however, requires that we cut down on busy-ness and ramp up our powers of observation—we slow down and look up. Making the transition from harried to attentive may feel uncomfortable at first, but we can take small actions each day to make paying attention easier. Instead of reading e-mail while talking on the phone, we might choose to concentrate only on our phone call. When focused, we find that we can *really* listen to our friend's voice on the phone, noticing the subtleties of her speech, the patterns of her words. We feel less stressed and more connected to both the task at hand and the world around us. As we practice slowing down and tuning in, we allow ourselves to receive priceless gifts that we otherwise might have missed: new ideas, deeper understanding, and greater peace.

Because we are individuals with unique backgrounds, beliefs, and experiences, each of us has a signature way of seeing the world. Our unique perspective is both vital to our creativity and nourishing to those around us. The more we practice paying attention, the more chances we have to discover our own special understanding of the world and use it to develop our personal creative style.

WATCHING FOR THE HELPING HAND

One of the best friends we'll meet along the creative journey isn't a person at all; it's more of a phenomenon, a presence. I like to call this the Creative Spirit. Some might call it God. Whatever we call it, the Creative Spirit is the benevolent force that created us, that invented nature, that built the beauty of space and time. During my own creative journey, I have noticed that when people set out to make positive changes in their lives, the Spirit is happy to help. Creative folks dig other creative folks, and the Creative Spirit is no exception. When we decide to embrace our creativity, the Spirit is our loudest cheerleader, welcoming us to the warmth of creativity and encouraging us in our endeavors.

This may sound like several pounds of baloney to some of us, and that's cool. There's no scientific evidence to back the Creative Spirit up, and I can't give you its e-mail address so you can ask it questions. But in the lives of creative people around the world, small miracles and coincidences pop up every day, courtesy of the Creative Spirit's Helping Hand. We might, say, have a creativity book to type but have no computer, and we find out a friend is selling her laptop for $100! We might decide we want to sing, and happen to meet a voice teacher on the bus. When we set out to do something with our creativity, the Spirit is known to get hyped and shoot some great opportunities our way. Part of the discipline of sustaining our creativity is to notice the Helping Hand and be willing to accept what it gives us.

Many of us have been taught that some things are too good to be true, and a kind Spirit helping us along might very well fall into this category. But as we will learn throughout this course, creating is more of a relationship than a solitary endeavor, a dance between our true selves and the Creative Spirit. Mary Shelley received the idea for *Frankenstein* in a dream, and used it to write a magnificent piece of literature. Michelangelo believed that David was already within the marble block, and he showed up each day to carve him out. Both of these creators noticed a small spark, an inspiring snap of the Helping Hand's fingers, and they put forth the effort to turn that spark into a work of art. Someday we, too, may be awoken with a glistening idea that must be realized. To prepare ourselves for this possibility, we practice keeping watch for tiny miracles today.

Just as we would take action if a brilliant movie script woke us up in the middle of the night, we must take action on the small gifts we are given each day. If you, the aspiring composer, see some dude writing music at the coffeeshop, that's your signal to grab that opportunity and go talk to him. He's not just there by chance; he's there for YOU. If you suddenly have a strong and unrelenting desire to attend a certain book signing, don't dismiss that feeling. GO! That book signing could be the event that alters the course of your life forever. As we move further along the creative path, we find that fewer and fewer things are mere coincidences. Lucky breaks and strong feelings are often signs that point us in the direction we need to go. We must train ourselves to recognize these signs, and to have the faith to follow them.

Your Unique Journey

As you embark on a creative quest, you may feel a strong urge to compare your progress to that of others around you. You may be pulled toward researching masters of your favorite art form, not to learn more about them, but to make note of how much further they are along the path than you are. As you listen to the people in our creativity group as they share, you may find yourself looking for the differences rather than the similarities: "Wow, she is so much more confident than I am. I don't know if I'll ever be that self-assured." This is exactly what the Critic wants you to do—to scare yourself back into hiding by manufacturing reasons that you're not good enough to create. Three words: Don't Do It!

Many of us have a bad habit of comparing ourselves to people who have traveled much further along the creative path than we have. We read articles about successful inventors and compare our few experiments to their long lists of ingenious creations. We view exhibitions of our favorite painter's work and frown at the thought of our tiny repertoire of half-finished canvases. If we're able to stay positive and focus the commonalities we share with accomplished creators, comparisons can be great motivational tools. Much of the time, though, our comparisons are of the "I could never do that" variety that leave us disheartened and disempowered. Comparing ourselves, fledgling creators, to seasoned masters is decidedly unfair, like having a shoe-tying contest between preschoolers and adults. Pitting absolute beginners against experts usually results in one thing and one thing only—the beginners' self-esteem taking a major beating. As young creators, we make our journey easier by focusing not on others' achievements, but on our own progress along the creative path.

In addition to downplaying our creative abilities by comparing ourselves to accomplished creators, many of us have an even deeper problem to conquer—our reluctance to celebrate our own talents and achievements. As we discussed in Chapter Two, we women are expert at nurturing others, but have incredible difficulty doing the same for ourselves. Similarly, many of us are able to clearly see others' power, promise, and potential, but have trouble noticing our own strengths. Even if we do make note of our victories, many of us have been taught that it's selfish to "toot our own horns." But remember, we creators need all the support we can get, starting with encouragement from within. When we fear that we don't measure up, instead of minimizing our talents like we may have done in the past, we must learn to compliment ourselves, celebrate our abilities, and embrace the experience of being our own biggest fans.

Creating isn't about measuring up to other people; it's about being true to ourselves. Although in times of uncertainty, we may be tempted to compare ourselves to other people on the path, we must remember that our creativity is unique, special, and completely our own. We must practice forging our own way, gauging our growth not with external comparisons, but in terms of our progress along our own path. We can learn that it's OK to pat ourselves on the back rather than wishing for others' encouragement, and shift our creative intentions from, "What will they think?" to "What do *I* need to say?" Perhaps the best way to sustain our creativity both in times of change and periods of stability is to toss out the yardstick and simply enjoy our own unique journey.

Creative Homework

1. Emotion Log - When we're walking the road toward embracing our creativity, our emotions are the scenery along the way. Each day, jot a little bit about the feelings you've felt that day. How do you feel during this process of learning to fully embrace your creativity? Are you feeling any of the Funky Four? If so, how are these emotions manifesting themselves in your life, and how are you using them? What are you enjoying about your journey?

2. Creative Habits - We read earlier about how perseverance can help us achieve our creative dreams. This week, figure out some ways you can integrate creative activities into your life each day. What can you do to make regular time to nurture your creativity and practice your favorite art form? How will you respond when you feel like pushing your creative activities aside? How can you make creativity a priority in your everyday life?

3. Declare Your Baggage - Resentments and regrets from the past can keep us from doing the things we want to do today. Here, we'll declare our baggage.

> **a.** List your regrets.
> **b.** List people and institutions you resent and why.
> **c.** Is anything else weighing down your carryon?
>   If so, write about it.
> **d.** Find a way to release this baggage from your life—burn the pages you've written, talk to the Creative Spirit, hide them in your Sack O' Woe—anything that will allow you to put your baggage aside so you can live in the here and now.

4. Attention - Pay attention to your life and your surroundings this week, using all five senses. Write a little each day about every aspect of a situation: how you feel, what you hear, what you taste, etc. Feel free to go hilariously overboard on detail, and let yourself run off on wild tangents if you feel the urge; but whatever you do, simply enjoy the experience of paying careful attention.

5. The Helping Hand - Be on the lookout for the Creative Spirit dancing around in your life this week. Gather evidence to prove it's there, guiding you, from the tiniest coincidences to the most intense torrent of emotion. As you notice little gifts popping up, practice putting aside your skepticism and allowing yourself to accept the present. What might the gift be trying to tell you? What will you choose to do with what you are given today?

6. Gathering the Troops - As we learned last week, it's important to have some true friends to help us on our creative journey. This week, think of the people in your life who make you feel happy, empowered, and strong. You may find it helpful to write a little bit about each person's gifts and specific ways they make your life better. Then, call up at least one of these people and chat. No, you are not too busy. Do it.

7. Compliments for You! - As many of us know, it can be *really* easy to find good things to say about others, and *really* hard to find good things to say about ourselves. Each day this week, write down at least one compliment about your progress on your creative journey. "I am so proud that I found time to write in my journal, even though today was busy!" is a good one. Or maybe, "I drew on a napkin today. Go me!" Read your compliments and smile; you're doing great. If the Critic pipes up, you know what to do. ☺

Chapter 4
Embracing Abundance

Goal: To begin to see how bountiful our world truly is, and to explore the spiritual side of creativity.

During the last three chapters, we've been working on getting to know ourselves better and learning to embrace the changes we've invited into our lives. In the next two chapters, we'll examine our views about the world in which we live. We may be unconsciously holding a negative, scarcity-based mentality, worrying that we don't have enough resources or talent to succeed as creative people. We may feel uncertain about where our ideas and security will come from when we're creative. Today, we'll begin to discover that we already have everything we need to succeed; all we need to do is learn to see that it's there!

The Abundance Mentality

Our society tends to operate on a scarcity mentality. From the endless supply of bad news to advertisements telling us we don't have enough, we tend to focus on what we lack and forget what we have. Even the misconceptions about creativity we explored in Chapter One are based on a scarcity mentality—we worry that if we find fulfillment by doing something we love, we'll have to give up other things that are important to us. A scarcity mentality tells us that life is characterized by lack, that there aren't enough opportunities to go around. When we adhere to this mentality, life becomes a scary place; we feel as if we're in constant competition for limited resources, we grow anxious about the future, and we become willing to tolerate less-than-ideal situations because we're afraid that they're the best we can get.

An abundance mentality, on the other hand, says that there are plenty of supplies, plenty of chances, plenty of opportunities in our lives. When we shift our mindsets from scarcity to abundance, we discover a greater sense of freedom. We find it easier to try new things and make mistakes because we know that we'll have many more chances to learn, grow, and succeed. Life transforms from a series of worries into a wealth of opportunities. Focusing on abundance enables us to explore our interests and take healthy risks while having faith that we'll be taken care of. As we continue on our journey, we'll find that we must be able to experiment and take chances to succeed creatively, and seeing the glass half full makes doing these things much easier.

FOUR WAYS TO FOSTER AN ATTITUDE OF ABUNDANCE

1. Shift your focus. What we focus on, we will see in the world. When we focus on our lack of creative experience, trying to create feels difficult and frustrating. But when we concentrate on making progress and finding ways to strengthen our creativity, we find that being creative isn't so hard.

2. Make a gratitude list. When we get stuck harping on what we don't have, it's helpful to take a minute to list what we DO have. Just sit down and list a few things you're grateful for today—your friends, your family, your pet, your car. Making a gratitude list can turn a rotten mood into a happy one pretty quickly, simply because it reminds us of all the richness in our lives that we find so easy to forget.

3. Go on a scarcity diet. What activates your scarcity mindset? Looking at the horribly expensive clothing in *Vogue*? Hearing the latest depressing stock market trends on the news? Hanging around certain people? Try restricting these things just like you'd restrict calories on a diet. Which of your friends are really upbeat, positive, and grateful for what they have? Hang out with them. Read magazines that don't advertise million-dollar shoes. When we're surrounded with abundance, it's easy to develop a positive mindset.

4. Look for little bits of abundance. While it's rare to find millions of dollars sitting on the sidewalk, it's common to encounter little bits of abundance scattered throughout our lives—finding a quarter on the floor, hearing from a good friend unexpectedly, arriving at work to find someone's brought a box of doughnuts. When we train ourselves to notice these small gifts, it becomes easier for us to allow larger blessings to enter our lives.

If we live in scarcity-based anxiety, we can worry ourselves right out of creating. If we want to dance, a scarcity mentality might tell us, "There are SO many good dancers out there; I'll never make it." This kind of lack-based thinking not only makes it hard for us to succeed in our endeavors, it can keep us from getting started on them at all. On the other hand, an abundance mentality says, "There's plenty of room for me in the world of dance!" and inspires us to get to work on achieving our creative dreams. When we focus on abundance, acting on our creative desires becomes a much easier task. Thinking abundantly, we can hear creativity's call and answer it confidently.

> *Without faith, nothing is possible.*
> *With it, nothing is impossible.*
>
> -Mary McLeod Bethune

God and Creativity

When we create, it's common to experience a feeling of flow, a profound focusing during which time seems to stand still and we lose track of our worries and cares. We are fully enmeshed with the divine in intense yet gleeful play. In these moments of flow, we catch a glimpse of who we truly are, and what creativity truly is. We are both creations and creators, masterworks of the Spirit who are capable of making creations of our own. Creativity is not simply a skill or talent; it's a capability we share with the Creative Spirit and the rest of humankind. When we create, we take off our masks and allow our true selves to dance with the Spirit. The energy of the dance flows through us, and we embrace it, celebrate it, and shape it into our own unique gift to the world.

The medium in which we create doesn't really matter; the Creative Spirit will partner with us to do something as involved as composing a symphony or as simple as solving an everyday problem at the office. We don't have to practice any specific religion or adhere to any certain spiritual principles to create with the Spirit. We don't have to be a particular age, race, gender, or nationality. We all have the ability to create simply because we are human, designed by the Creative Spirit to be creative ourselves. When we do the work to rid ourselves of negative beliefs, open our minds to new ideas, and embrace our authentic selves, we open ourselves to fulfill our uniquely human potential—to turn our creative desires into reality.

Whatever our spiritual beliefs are, it's difficult to doubt the presence of the divine in the creative process. Walking the creative path requires tremendous amounts of honesty, faith, acceptance, and surrender, all common tools that accompany spiritual quests. Likewise, creative works themselves often bear the hallmarks of spirituality, pushing us past our perceived limits and raising more questions than they answer. Although the divine can be difficult to understand, allowing it into our creative endeavors tends to make creating *easier*. The Creative Spirit is the spark, the spirit of play that helps us create in an effortless flow. When we acknowledge the work of this powerful force in our lives, we are able to dip into an endless supply of ideas and inspiration. We no longer have to struggle to think things up; we can spend our time taking things down, gathering ideas and shaping them into unique creations.

In this section of the course, it's important that we take a closer look at our spiritual views and experiences, and examine them to see how they influence our creative understanding. We may discover that we haven't explored God's creative side very much, or that we sometimes get God's will and society's will mixed up. Either way, we're in for an exciting ride. We have learned much about ourselves, and now we're ready to examine the strongest force for creativity in the universe. I encourage you to keep an open mind and a spirit of exploration as you learn more about the spiritual side of creativity.

THE CREATIVE SPIRIT AND ABUNDANCE

Earlier, we had a brief introduction to the Creative Spirit, a being who is a creator itself, who gave us our creativity, and who supports us in our endeavors to embrace our true roles as creative beings. The Creative Spirit and abundance are inseparable partners; after all, the Spirit often reveals itself by showering us with little miracles. If we learn to trust the Spirit, we will find that we're well taken care of. The Creative Spirit is a "Yes We Can" kind of being. With its support, yes we can take a six-month sabbatical to write our novel and still pay the rent. Keeping our eyes on the Helping Hand, yes we can enjoy a rich supply of good ideas.

Much of the time, we don't even consider how powerful the Creative Spirit truly is. This is the force that created both the boundless depths of outer space and the detailed intricacies of the human circulatory system and the laws that govern subatomic particles. It is immensely, unimaginably powerful, and has the potential to literally move mountains. The Creative Spirit is the embodiment of abundance. It has plenty of money, tons of great ideas, and an endless supply of friends and resources to share with us. All we have to do is pay attention and we can learn how to tap into these resources.

Many of us bar ourselves from accepting the Spirit's generous gifts with our own limited ideas of what's possible in our lives. Thinking from a scarcity mindset, it's common for us to hear the voice of the Spirit and begin following it toward magnificent opportunities, only to throw on the brakes by saying the message is crazy or too good to be true. Sometimes we may miss chances because we limit our attention to certain messengers; for example, we wait anxiously by the phone for the club owner to call us back, while we ignore the well-connected booking agent we meet at our kids' ballgame. On the creative path, learning to trust the Spirit and pay attention to where it's leading us is of utmost importance. The Spirit is bountiful and willing to help us; when we let go of our expectations and limits, we open ourselves to receive that help.

The Spirit also has an abundance of information that we don't have; it sees the big picture. Over time, we notice that when we follow the Spirit, we always end up in the right place. The small voice of the Creative Spirit tends to lead us toward inside information. We may not know why we're being called to do something, but we slowly discover the details as we move forward. When we practice trusting where we're being led, we can find a wealth of ideas, supplies, and understanding we otherwise would have missed. Over time, we find that listening to the Spirit enhances not only our creativity, but our everyday lives as well.

GOD'S WILL VS. SOCIETY'S WILL

Our world and the spiritual realm are very different places. Here, we're regularly exposed to myths of self-sufficiency, money as security, and lack. These myths are poisonous to our creativity. Working as an island can quickly dry out our flow of ideas, and we need only look at certain celebrities to see that it's easy to have tons of money and be creatively barren. And as we've already learned, a mindset focused on scarcity can worry us right out of creating. In the spiritual realm, however, creativity is a fruitful partnership, the Spirit is our security, and we know there's always enough. Here, we'll talk values—those that support our creativity and those that hold it back.

Society and the Creative Spirit are frequently at odds in terms of values. Society says that working hard and never asking for help is good. Suffering each day at a terrible job means we have "dedication." Being a "yes" person, AKA letting people walk all over us, is considered desirable. Dealing with problems ourselves, rather than sharing them with our friends, means we're strong. In my experience, I've found that these things are not true. For years, I taught school—a job that never quite fit. I felt completely out of place, but took people's advice and "hung in there" because I was "making a difference" in my "noble profession." As job stress made me physically sick and mentally spent, I began hearing a voice saying, "Christina, LEAVE!" Eventually, I followed that voice, that still, small voice of the divine. I felt better than I had in years, genuinely happy. My dried-up creative juices began to flow again, and my health turned around. Society, however, lamented, "But you had TENURE! Why couldn't you just do another year FOR THE KIDS??" I was called by God and I followed. Society roundly disapproved.

Another disconnect between society and spirituality concerns our source of security. Although we've all heard about depending on God, many of us were raised to believe that money is the real source of security. To people conditioned to see money as security, the idea of trusting the divine to care for us seems foolish and unrealistic. This conditioning is a direct result of the scarcity mentality. Worried that there's not enough to go around, we only trust stuff that we can see, touch, and stick in our wallets. The problem is, money is a finite, human-made product with limited purchasing power—no amount of money can buy love, happiness, or creative freedom. However, when we depend on the Spirit, we have an infinite supply—of time, ideas, and even cash. Focusing on our spiritual health can give us things that money can't buy, like quality time with loved ones and the joy of honoring our calling. We're warned that if we don't put stock in money, we'll starve. But the truth is, when we place our trust in things other than money, we are well-fed indeed.

As we live our lives, we can choose to conform to society's way of scarcity and limitations, or to follow the abundant and open path of the Creative Spirit. It may be helpful to envision society's path and the spiritual path as examples, and determine which example we'd most like to follow. Do we want to be more like the Creative Spirit who invented the beauty of the universe, or society which created the negative nightly news? The Spirit who invites us to create with reckless abandon, or society which invites us to do what we're told?

All this talk about transcending society's values and depending on some invisible creative force to care for us may sound pretty scary. We may worry that the author will break out the Kool-Aid and start chanting about returning to the mothership in the next chapter. We may fear that we must change all our beliefs to be creative. The answer: Absolutely not. All we have to do is look at our beliefs and ask, "Does this empower me to reach my creative potential? Or, does this make me feel like I'm foolish for following my dreams?" We can choose to let go of beliefs that push us down, and live by those that strengthen us.

Gratitude

Perhaps one of the best ways to change our perspective on life is to practice gratitude. We humans are adept at seeing the gloomy side of the street, expert at staring at the shadow instead of the sunlight. When we make a conscious decision to count our blessings instead of our woes, we find that we experience a profound shift in our attitudes about the availability of good things in our world. Since many of the myths that keep us from our creativity are scarcity-based, making the effort to see the world from a more positive perspective can go a long way toward blasting through creative blockage.

Practicing gratitude can be very simple. We can start by making a daily gratitude list. Each day, make a commitment to write down several things you are grateful for. These don't have to be big or expensive things; they just have to be blessings in your life. A sample list might look like:

> ### Today I'm thankful for:
> *My home*
> *My family*
> *My health*
> *My job*

Once we've written a bit, it's helpful to dig a little deeper and think about why we're thankful for the things we've listed. What do we love about our families? What are some things we cherish about our homes, jobs, and friends? Gratitude and attention go hand in hand, and as we know, paying attention can turn a trickle of thoughts into a raging river of ideas. We can spend each day hunting for things we're grateful for, and challenge ourselves to notice even the smallest blessings. My list might look like this:

> **I'm so grateful for our house; it's such a relaxing place!**
>
> **Today Andrew e-mailed me a cool video he knew I'd like! Priceless!**
>
> **I cherish the times when Velvet sleeps on our feet at night.**
>
> **I am so happy that I can touch my toes!**
>
> **My trombone slide worked so smoothly today! Thank God!**

In the tiny details of our lives is where the true power of gratitude lies, simply because when we sit down and think about it, we have an infinite number of little things to be grateful for. When we notice these things, we open up a paradox. We begin to feel more comfortable with our lives just as they are, but at the same time we feel more empowered to make changes and take healthy risks. We find ourselves spending less time wishing to win the lottery and more time celebrating the gifts we have today. But in appreciating our gifts, we tend to find new possibilities, fresh ideas, and exciting opportunities that can bring us further success.

When we stand back and appreciate what's in front of us, we may find that we fall in love. As we come to know our life more deeply, we realize that it's something we don't want to be without. The more little things we appreciate, the more dear our lives become to us, the more passionate we are about our existence. And passion gives birth to a wellspring of ideas. When we're wishy-washy and whatever, being bored, detached, and idealess is the norm. However, when we love something intensely, our ideas flow effortlessly and there is always something to joyfully do. Gratitude is a small mindset shift that can cause us to fall madly in love with our lives. Our own lives can be our muse, our raging river of ideas.

Cultivating an attitude of gratitude takes practice, because our brains are creatures of habit. The neural pathways we use most often grow stronger and more efficient—each time we react a certain way, that path gets a fresh layer of myelin "pavement." Over time, when faced with which route to take, the brain is more likely to take the beautifully-paved highways over the tiny dirt trails that we rarely use. We must ask ourselves, is grateful thinking a highway in our minds, or a scrawny little footpath? If we are used to seeing our lives in terms of lack, practicing gratitude literally blazes new trails in our minds. When we think of our blessings, we begin clearing the brush off those unused positive pathways. Each time we think positively, we whack down a few more weeds. Just as clearing a course through a dense forest is time consuming, fortifying patterns of positive, grateful thinking takes deliberate and sustained effort.

A Little More On Fear

When we work on shifting our mindsets and examining our views on life, we push past the boundaries of our comfort zones to explore new territory. Just as the pioneers faced attackers on their westward journeys, we may easily be ambushed by fear as we try new things. Unfortunately, it's not always easy to identify fear for what it really is. Like the Critic with its numerous styles of nagging, fear wears many disguises to try to weasel its way into our lives. When we learn to be on the lookout for the different costumes fear might don, we can more easily detect it and see how it's operating in our lives. Here are some of the most common disguises fear wears when it tries to sneak into the lives of creative people:

EIGHT COMMON DISGUISES FOR FEAR:

1. Needing to be in control

2. Tolerating unhealthy situations and people

3. Being resistant to change

4. Creating unnecessary clutter, busy-ness, or drama

5. Making excuses; rationalizing

6. Avoiding the problem

7. Trying to manipulate others

8. Procrastinating

The Artist/The Messenger

According to popular misconceptions, creating involves sitting alone and thinking things up out of thin air. In reality, creating is a relationship, an intimate interaction between our innermost selves and the Creative Spirit. We creative people are fields, and the Creative Spirit is the wind carrying the seeds—the ideas, inspirations, and *Eureka!* moments. When we strengthen our creative abilities, we're readying ourselves not to think up, but to receive and realize. We prepare our soil, fertilize it, and open it to the possibility of growth. We have faith that the wind will blow in seeds of inspiration and we keep watch for these seeds to arrive. We listen and wait for the Creative Spirit, and when its ideas come blowing by, we catch them, draw them in, cover them up, and encourage them to grow. Trusted to our care, the seeds/ideas grow into lush and beautiful works of art, pieces of music, theories of science. The creative person is a messenger, receiving information and joyfully carrying it into the world for all to see.

Over the past four chapters, we have been preparing our fields to receive the Creative Spirit. We have pulled out the weeds of misunderstanding, cleared our land of the pollution of baggage and anxiety, and enriched our soil with empowering affirmations. When we learn to respect ourselves and our ideas, to accept the small gifts the Spirit sends us, and to have faith that creativity is possible, something beautiful happens. We begin to receive. We align ourselves with an inexhaustible flow of inspiration—brilliant closing arguments, books, plays, legislation, curriculum, ballets, sonatas, recipes, plans are all there for the taking. All we have to do is take hold of them and nurture them into fruition. This flow is never-ending, and at times the Creative Spirit will scatter showers of possibility over vast areas of our lives.

We can catch these raindrops of opportunity by paying attention and listening. When we pay attention, we become more attuned to the world around us. When we listen, we tap into our partnership with the Creative Spirit. With our minds and senses open to receive, we allow the possibility of that perfect spark, that brilliant idea, to come through. Once we receive that idea, we are free to realize it using our own unique personality and gifts. As messengers, we don't have to worry about creating the next great masterwork or fret over what everyone might think of what we make. We simply listen and make the work that needs to happen, happen.

Creative Homework

1. Sensing Abundance - Take a few minutes to think about what abundance looks, feels, sounds, and smells like. As you complete the following sentences, allow yourself to vividly imagine abundance using each of your senses, and enjoy your daydream of overflowing bounty.

To me, abundance...
looks like_____
sounds like_____
smells like_____
tastes like_____
feels like_____

2. Examining Our Ideas About Divine Abundance - Take some time this week to write about the Creative Spirit in terms of abundance. What is some evidence that the Spirit is bountiful and generous? Think about nature, the cosmos, and your own experiences. What is some evidence that the Spirit is stingy? When the Spirit seems stingy, is it really *us* imposing limitations?

3. Abundance Reminders - We have plenty of reminders of the scarcity mentality surrounding us each day; why not make some reminders of abundance? Get some paper and art supplies and make your own signs to remind you of the abundant side of life. Make your signs say whatever you want them to say, and stick them in places where you'll see them regularly. "Everything's gonna be OK!" on your bathroom mirror. "I have plenty of time," on your desk. "We are blessed with lots of good food," by the fridge.

4. Your Higher Power - This week, take some time to write about God. Who or what is God to you? What does God value and enjoy? What does God envision for your life? If these questions are tough to answer, it may be helpful to think first of what God *isn't* and what God *doesn't* value, enjoy, and want for you. Don't censor yourself for fear of what other people might think. Write, and enjoy exploring your personal spirituality.

5. Gratitude List - Sometime each day this week, sit down and make a gratitude list. You can write it, think about it, or tell another person the things you're grateful for. You can use the guidelines earlier in the chapter if you need help getting started. The important thing is to consciously take time to blaze new trails of positive, grateful thinking in your mind.

> **5a.** Whenever you find yourself down in the dumps and thinking negatively, stop right then and there and make a gratitude list. How does this mindset shift affect your mood?

6. Fear Detectives - Sometimes, simply acknowledging feelings of fear can strip them of their power. Over the next week, sleuth around your life looking for fear in its various disguises. What ways does fear take form in your life? What can you do to deal with these fears?

7. Good Habits Checkpoint - How are you doing with your good creative habits this week? Take a few minutes to write about how practicing creative habits can bring abundance into your life.

Chapter 5
Embracing Possibility

Goal: To learn to view the world as a place of promise and potential, and lessen our perceived limitations.

The Possibility of Being Enough

One of the most deep-seated fears many of us have is that we're not enough. We're not smart enough to go back to school, not pretty enough to ask the hot guy out, not talented enough to sing in a band. To successfully live a creative life, we must slowly build a sense of possibility and promise within ourselves, while ridding ourselves of nagging thoughts that tell us we're inadequate.

PERFECTIONISM

At its core, perfectionism is driven by this fear of inadequacy. Afraid that we don't have enough talent, smarts, or anything else we think people want, we try to compensate for our perceived lack by trying to do things perfectly. Although perfectionism may seem like striving to do our best, it tends to bring out our worst traits: fear and self-centeredness. We may try to call perfectionism by different names, like making sure our project is ready, having high standards, or being detail-oriented, but in truth, perfectionism is simply harmful, a lump of creative kryptonite.

Although perfectionism may appear like a singular focus on our work, in reality it's a focus on what people might *think* of our work. When we practice perfectionism, we fix our eyes so firmly on the future that we lose sight of the beauty and promise our work holds today. While creative play is a productive flow, fearful perfectionism is a stifling quicksand of insignificant details. Fearful of others' criticism, we anxiously obsess over tiny trivialities and compulsively flail around in details until our project suffocates. Practicing perfectionism, we rework our story so many times that we forget what we wanted to say in the first place. We fret so hard about playing in tune that we miss half our notes. Instead of creating with ease and freedom, we allow a ball and chain of fear to break our flow.

When we engage in perfectionism, it's often because the Critic has found a way behind our Purple Velvet Rope. We may find we've been worrying too much about the future, or haven't been listening to our Inner Artist; either way, we've left our Rope unguarded. When we neglect our Rope and indulge in self-doubt, the Critic will try to jump over and give its opinion on our work. If fear tosses us into a quicksand of details, the Critic stirs up a hailstorm, pelting us with insults, doubts, and outright lies— anything that might separate us from our creative work. Remember, the Critic is a survival instinct, not an artistic one. It wants things to be perfect—perfectly safe, perfectly normal, perfectly sterile—so our tribe won't reject us and toss us out into the wilderness. The Critic is a constant worrier who places safety over self-expression; if we allow the Critic to grab our ear, its anxiety can easily grow contagious and sicken our work.

As women, perfectionism can hit home for us in an intense and familiar way. Sometimes it seems like everywhere we go, we're confronted with images of "perfect" women. Magazines are full of photographs of impossibly gorgeous women wearing outfits that would take many of us a year's salary to afford. Talk shows feature beautiful celebrities who seem to expertly balance marriage, family, career, and friends while looking perfect doing it. There are even shows devoted to making fun of people who don't dress stylishly/perfectly enough! When we're pelted from all sides with overly-high standards anyway, taking on a new endeavor like a creative discipline can double the pressure we feel to be flawless.

Fortunately, we don't have to be dominated by a quest for perfection. Perfectionism is somewhat like a disease, with causes (fear of criticism, focusing on "what ifs"), symptoms (anxiety, obsession, beating ourselves up), and treatments (which we'll discuss on the next page). While perfectionism may take a while to subside, and may rear its ugly head at various times throughout our lives, it is possible to set it aside and focus on cultivating healthy self-acceptance. Here are five simple actions we can take to treat our perfection-itis:

FIVE WAYS TO STOP PERFECTIONISM IN ITS TRACKS

1. STOP! If you feel yourself slipping into perfectionism quicksand, put down whatever you're working on and do something else. Perfectionism is an obsessive-compulsive activity; sometimes a simple change of scenery can help us break the cycle and free ourselves from the quicksand's grip.

2. Stay in the now. Perfectionism is often triggered when we switch our focus from "what is" to "what if?" People are built to live in the present, not in the future. When we try to play the prophet and figure out what others might think, all we do is drive ourselves crazy trying to know the unknowable. When we stay in the now, we free ourselves to do what we CAN do, our creative work!

3. Express your gratitude. Gratitude lists are not only mood lifters, but perfectionism busters as well. Try writing a list of things you love. Now ask yourself, "How many things on this list are perfect?" You'll quickly realize the answer is *none*, but you cherish these things nonetheless. You can even make gratitude lists about your creative projects; they'll help you see the strengths in your work that you may tend to overlook.

4. Connect with the divine. We can look to our partnership with the Spirit for inspiration to appreciate ourselves as we are. To create, we need only show up as our honest and true selves. The Spirit didn't pick some "perfect" person out there to create your latest project. It chose YOU. Why worry what other people think, when the Creative Spirit loves you just the way you are?

5. Use affirmations. We may be getting tired of reading about affirmations, but all the same, they work! The more we surround ourselves with positive truths, the easier it becomes to let go of perfectionism's fearful lies.

NO PEDESTALS ALLOWED

One thing that turns me off of fellow musicians faster than anything else is when they sit around and talk about good players as if they're superhuman titans of the musical arts. Why do I hate this so much? Because it sets up an "us" and "them" mentality in which "they" are always much more musical, much more capable, and much better players than "we" can ever hope to be. Putting any other human being up on a pedestal can quickly and thoroughly poison our creativity.

The fact of the matter is, the greatest artists, musicians, filmmakers, etc. in the world share something vital with us; they are people. Accomplished creative people were made by the same Spirit who made us, and they have the same basic needs and capabilities that we do. The only difference between us is what we've done with our time. People who have made their mark on the world generally have done it through practice, hard work, and more practice. Frida Kahlo once practiced drawing lines. Yo-Yo Ma once practiced moving his bow across the strings. The only thing that separates us from these two great artists is many hours of practice. There isn't something special in the water that great artists drink, there is just a path that they've committed to following. We can follow that path, too.

When we place people on pedestals, we automatically place ourselves at a lower elevation. Putting fellow creators far above us makes us feel like there's no way we can ever measure up. However, there's no "measuring up" about creativity; creative people don't grow tall, we just walk far. Creative people of all stripes are merely human beings walking a path. Now that we've set our feet on the creative path as well, fellow creators around the world, even the "great" ones, are our brothers and sisters. They understand how it feels to do what we're doing, and we're getting a glimpse of what it's like to be them. When we set ourselves on equal footing with others, we establish a sense of possibility around our creativity that gives us the strength to continue, to commit, and to excel.

The Possibility of Being in Balance

One element that can make a creative life much more pleasant and productive is achieving a sense of balance. As creative people, we have specific needs that we must honor; however, we also have other responsibilities that deserve our attention. Working to achieve balance in our lives can keep our creativity, our relationships, and our selves healthy.

OUR NEEDS AS CREATIVE PEOPLE

To maintain our creative health, we have certain requirements that need to be filled. So far on our journey, we've already had to make room in our lives for new creativity-boosting habits, as well as become willing to let go of snares that hold our creativity back. As we continue on our journey, we'll find that the good habits we've formed aren't just for use during the eight weeks of this course, but can enrich and enliven our lives for as long as we practice them. The more time we spend with our Inner Artist, the stronger our bond will grow, and the more freely our ideas will flow. The better we care for ourselves, the more confident we will feel. The more we nurture our creativity, the more fruitful our creative practice will become.

Perhaps creative people's most common requirement is Personal Time. The creative mind generates ideas in a sometimes torrential flow, and a healthy Inner Artist regularly sends out strong, persistent urges to create: "Come on, it's time to play!!" Neglecting to process our ideas creates a backlog of stale thoughts in our minds, and ignoring the urge to play depletes our supply of creative fuel. Our creative machinery grinds to a halt. We feel deprived, frazzled, and frustrated, especially when others' demands try to find their way into our already full minds. However, when we take even a few minutes alone each day to reflect and play, we keep our creativity healthy and robust.

Personal Time allows us to strengthen our connections with the Inner Artist and the Creative Spirit, two entities that are vital to our creative health. The closer we are to the Artist and Spirit, the easier we can jump into the creative flow. But although these two friends are always nearby, we can easily fall out of touch if we don't spend quality time with them. Our Personal Time frees us from the distractions and opinions of other people, allowing us to lose ourselves in play with our Inner Artist and more fully listen for the guidance of the Creative Spirit. Alone with the Artist and Spirit, we find creative joy and peace.

Just as we need Personal Time away from outside pressures, it can also be important to know when to *add* a bit of stimulation to our creative process. Because many creative people don't have bosses, we must supply our own motivation to turn ideas into finished works. We may need to set a deadline to keep our project moving, or decide the best motivation is to take a break and see a play. The way we make decisions like these is to learn more about ourselves—how we think, how we work, and how best to keep our creativity flowing. To achieve creative success, we must consider ourselves worthy of our own attention, and strive to keep getting to know ourselves better. Since finishing projects requires a deep understanding of how we do things, making time to learn more about our working style is vital to sustaining our creativity.

Another creative necessity is the possibility of new experiences. Having novel adventures doesn't have to be expensive or time consuming; all we need is a willingness to try new things. Our new experiences can be as small as taking a different route home from work or listening to a new radio station, or as grand as taking an extended vacation to a place we've never been. No matter how we approach it, adding variety to our lives brings creative refreshment. People are creatures of habit down to the structure of our brains. When we expose ourselves to fresh scenery and unique perspectives, we challenge our brains to think differently and make exciting new connections.

Lastly, as creative beings we need all the support we can get. You may have noticed that much of the work we're doing in this course has to do with personal development: affirmations, positive thinking, boundary-setting. We do this work because our need for support begins with ourselves. To fully embrace our creativity, we must believe in our ideas and our capacity to bring them to fruition, and we must develop the courage to be true to ourselves. By strengthening our sense of self and practicing healthy habits, we can become our own best friends, an always-open waffle shop of encouragement. In addition to believing in ourselves, it's helpful to have others who believe in and support us as well. People who truly understand us may be few and far between, but nurturing relationships with supportive friends can make our creativity, and our lives in general, much richer.

> *You see things; and you say, "Why?" But I dream things that never were; and I say, "Why not?"*
>
> -George Bernard Shaw

THE DANGERS OF PEOPLE PLEASING

Unfortunately, many of creativekind's basic needs may be relegated to the "fluff" category in some people's lives. "Time alone? But you need to spend time with your kids! New experiences? You need to just be happy with what you have!" Sadly, it's common to encounter folks who don't understand where we're coming from, and these people may even be our loved ones. It can be difficult to stand up for our creative needs when people around us think we're being weird or selfish, and when the pressure to fulfill society's expectations feels like a crushing weight on our shoulders.

One way that many of us respond to this pressure is to buckle, saying, "I'd like to do something creative today, but everyone else *needs* me!" and begin walking down the dangerous avenue of people pleasing. In our efforts to make our loved ones happy, we devote substantial amounts of energy to being good wives, good mothers and good friends. When we people-please, we're good to everyone but ourselves! Although we may feel a nagging urge to give ourselves some much needed TLC, we ignore it in favor of doing what others want us to do. We may engage in people pleasing because we have low self-confidence, because we don't want to appear selfish, or to avoid catching grief from others for going against the flow. Just as people pleasing has a number of possible causes, it also takes many forms, including:

> **Consistently putting others' desires before our own**
>
> **Doing things because we think we should**
>
> **Saying "yes" when we really want to say "no"**
>
> **Constantly worrying about what others think of us**
>
> **Feeling afraid to share our opinions and ideas**
>
> **Letting others make our decisions for us**
>
> **Going with others' plans even when we don't want to**
>
> **Feeling unable to make decisions on our own**

We sabotage our creativity when we sacrifice our creative desires to please others. Perhaps we forego taking an exciting art class because it means we'll miss some of our daughter's ballgames, or cancel plans to attend a creative retreat because our boyfriend thinks it's weird. Making sacrifices sometimes is necessary, but if we continually place our creativity on the back burner to suit others, we begin to harm our Inner Artist. Love and attention are food and water to our Artist. Every time we neglect her needs, our Artist goes hungry. Over time, she begins to starve. And just like a starving person, the longer food is withheld the faster she withers away, taking our creativity along with her.

People pleasing can be a deep-seated problem that is difficult to recognize and overcome; learning how to be kind to others and ourselves at the same time can be as tricky as walking a tightrope. The good news is that achieving balance between ourselves and the people around us is entirely possible. As we move further into our journey, we'll continue to discuss ways to balance a healthy respect for ourselves with our responsibilities to others.

BALANCING US AND THEM

As creative people, we need Personal Time to devote to our creative pursuits, yet we have families, friends, and responsibilities that demand our attention as well. It's easy to make the mistake of trying to do one or the other—shutting everyone out and just being alone, or blowing off our creative desires so we can do what others want us to do. However, a better way to go about this is through balance and communication.

Sitting down and talking calmly and positively with family and friends can go a long way toward helping us balance our own needs with those of our loved ones. It's very common for others to voice their expectations to us—"Honey, aren't you going to vacuum today?"—but often, we hesitate to let others know what we expect of them. Voicing our expectations can be difficult, especially if we were raised to keep quiet and go with the flow. However, defining our boundaries and showing others how we want to be treated can encourage our loved ones to treat us with greater thoughtfulness and respect.

When we're willing to give up what we love for others, people will like us; after all, we're giving them what they want. But will they respect us? Hardly. Rather, they will see what else they can eek out of us. When we let others know that our creative commitments will not be changed to suit their whims, we create the possibility for an entirely different result. People may complain when we first establish boundaries around our creativity (because they're no longer calling the shots), but over time they'll begin to view us as stronger people whose needs are worthy of their consideration. It is possible to have healthy, enduring relationships with others and still be true to ourselves. When we make a commitment to set healthy boundaries and stick up for ourselves, we allow our creativity and confidence to flourish.

In dealing with other people, one problem we may encounter is our own assumptions. If we haven't done many creative activities before, we may assume that our loved ones think we're strange and don't like what we're doing. We may put off doing creative things at home because we're certain that our loved ones will make fun of us or disapprove; after all, only weirdos do creative stuff, right? We can easily blow assumptions up in our minds until we're convinced that everyone's out to get us, but the remedy to this problem is just as simple. We find out the truth. If we're hesitant to create because we think our loved ones don't like it, our top priority should be to talk with our loved ones and learn how they *really* feel. Often, we'll be relieved to find supportive people who are excited about our new endeavors.

> *No person is your friend who demands your silence, or denies your right to grow.*
>
> -Alice Walker

DISCUSSING YOUR CREATIVE NEEDS WITH LOVED ONES

Although communicating our needs and boundaries to other people won't ensure that they'll become totally open-minded and excited about our creativity, it's definitely something that's worth a try. When we make the effort to explain our creative pursuits to others and help them understand us better, we invite them to be a part of our journey, and establish guidelines that show people how we want to be treated.

1. Get to the bottom of the problem. Before you sit down with your loved ones for a chat, ask yourself, "Do my loved ones really have a problem with my creativity, or am I just *assuming* they do?" Have people said anything that makes you feel like they resent your new creative ventures, or are you just afraid they might? If you're not sure, try asking! You might start a great conversation, or uncover some problems to work on solving.

2. Make an appointment. Planning a specific time to talk to your loved ones about your creative endeavors can go a long way toward making the interaction more positive and effective. Try to find a quiet time when not much is going on, and schedule your meeting in advance so that nobody's caught off guard.

3. Make a plan. Before you and your loved ones sit down to talk, think ahead about your audience and what you want to tell them. Is your family excited for you and interested in hearing more about what you're doing? Or is there someone who's giving you a hard time with whom you'd like to discuss your boundaries? When you plan ahead, you'll be better prepared to communicate your message in a clear and powerful way.

4. Listen. When we communicate, we both speak and listen—we allow our loved ones to express themselves as well. Listening to those who may not "get" what we're doing can be frustrating, especially if we've become passionate about making creativity part of our lives. However, listening can help us understand others' confusion and provide an opportunity for us to clear up their misconceptions surrounding creativity.

As we've discussed previously, there will always be people who use shame to try to make us be and do what makes THEM comfortable. If we stand up for our creativity and honor our true desires, odds are we'll meet up with at least one of these people on our creative journey. It might be the old friend who coldly remarks,

"You've changed," or a coworker who makes a sour face when we present one of our new ideas. We all want people to like us, and facing others' disapproval can feel absolutely rotten. However, we can use tools like comforting our Inner Artist, talking to trusted friends, and saying affirmations to lessen the sting of such encounters.

The Possibility of a Creative Life

When we were kids, we had wild dreams of accomplishing things that many adults consider impossible—dreams of being cowgirls, astronauts, supermodels, and world-famous athletes. As we grew up and experienced some of life's trials, we slowly left our big audacious dreams behind and tied a leash of "reality" around our sense of possibility. This leash is what holds us back from achieving our creative potential! We don't allow ourselves to dream exciting, extravagant dreams. We pull the leash back when a truly incredible idea starts to emerge. To start turning our creative desires into reality, we need to remove the leash and give ourselves permission to dream again. Today we can reawaken our fantasies and renew our sense of possibility. Many of the tools we've learned in this course are aimed at doing just that—restoring our sense of possibility and passion.

Imagine if a person from the Stone Age traveled through time and visited our modern world. He's used to sleeping on the ground, spending all day hunting for his dinner, and fighting off attackers with primitive stone tools. Imagine what he'd think of memory foam mattresses, supermarkets, and handguns! Our modern conveniences would blow his mind simply because they're far beyond his realm of possibility. Even people today are amazed by the changes in possibility that have occurred within their lifetimes. If you had told us kids back in the early 1980s that we'd have portable phones that could play music and take pictures, we would have said, "Impossible!" But today, these "impossible" machines are everywhere.

Our creative potential is the same way. Today, we may not see the possibilities that lie within us—the ideas stewing deep inside our minds, the dreams preparing to be awakened, the projects waiting to be realized. However, if we continue on our creative journey, even the wildest of our dreams may someday come into focus. The creative process is a gradual unveiling; as we continue to create, we discover ever greater depths of ability and promise within ourselves.

Creative Homework

1. Perfectionism Checkpoint - This week, be on the lookout for perfectionism in your life, and make note of it. How do you feel when you're subjecting yourself to overly high standards? What are some things you think you might be willing to try if you didn't have to do them perfectly?

> If you think you might have a problem with perfectionism and you want a more in-depth way of tackling it, check out:
>
> **http://www.livestrong.com/article/14702-overcoming-perfectionism**

2. People Pleasing Scoreboard - One easy way to reveal people pleasing behavior is to carefully watch your life and keep score. This week, keep a count of how many times you nurture yourself vs. how many times you nurture others. The score you end up with can be quite telling! Is it you-0, everyone else-10, or vice-versa? I enjoy going for an even tie (but then again, I'm a balance-loving Libra!)

> If you feel like people pleasing is a big problem in your life, you might want to learn more at:
>
> **http://www.earley.org/Patterns/people_pleaser.htm**

3. Reclaiming Your Dreams - What are some of the big, over-the-top dreams you had as a kid? What are some ideas you've had lately that you've dismissed as "too extravagant" or "too wild" or "impossible"? Write all of these down and imagine them coming true. What would your life be like if you auditioned for a play, or started having monthly concerts at your house? What is keeping you from acting on your dreams? Is there a simple action that you can take today to bring one of these dreams closer to reality?

4. The Great Talent Inventory - The first step in realizing your true potential is to uncover and eliminate negative beliefs about your capabilities. This week, write a list of your talents and abilities. What are you great at? What do you enjoy doing more than anything else? Now, write down any limits you believe your talents have. For example, your talent might be, "I can plan a killer party!" and your limitation might be, "But I'd never be good enough to plan a party for the president!" Just like you did with the Critic's objections, turn these limitations around. ("President Obama would have a ball at one of my fabulous parties!") When you're done, if your list of talents and capabilities sounds completely over-the-top, you've done your job.

***5. Ideation - (*Make sure you do this one!!*) Imagine you're living in a perfect world where you have infinite talent, time, and abilities. Every person is open-minded and kind, so you don't have to worry about criticism or doing everything perfectly. In this world, what are some things you'd create? These can be objects like a painting or sculpture, events like a party or class, or anything else you can think of. Write your ideas down quickly before your Critic can shoot them down, and read over them each day this week.

6. Good Habits Checkpoint - How did you do with incorporating healthy creative habits into your life this week? How has practicing creative habits affected your overall sense of possibility?

Chapter 6
The Strength to Begin

Goal: To move past barriers that hinder us from starting our projects, and discover ways to nurture our early creative efforts.

So far on our journey, we have laid a firm foundation upon which to build our creative endeavors. We have gilded ourselves with assurance and strength, and have learned to see the world in a more empowering light. Now, it's time to take the most difficult step in the creative process—to begin. Beginning is an act that can be fraught with emotions, a challenge that can tempt us to run back into hiding. This week, we'll unravel several difficulties involved in starting the creative process, and begin developing our own understanding of how to turn our ideas into reality.

Criticism

One of the main reasons people shy away from beginning creative projects is the possibility of criticism. As we've discussed earlier, society is expert at criticizing people, their abilities, and their creations. When we create something, we open ourselves up and allow others to scrutinize an honest expression of who we are. We are vulnerable, and vulnerability is outside many people's comfort zones entirely. In this section, we'll learn how to deal with criticism: the good kind, the bad kind, and the not-quite-there kind that exists only in the future.

The first thing to keep in mind about criticism is that it takes place at the END of a project. We may ask editors for feedback as our book nears completion, or send our finished CD to a music magazine to be reviewed, but there's no place for criticism in the formative stages of our work. Like the first few years of a child's life, the early stages of creative projects are all about experimenting, exploring, and playing. Just as nagging caretakers can make small children nervous and afraid, early criticism can stunt our young projects' growth. To protect our growing projects, we store the reality of criticism in the back of our minds, away from our current thoughts. We refrain from fantasizing about feedback. We stop trying to predict what people will say. When we keep the possibility of criticism where it belongs—in the future—we enable ourselves to work in the here and now.

While it's common to fret over future criticism, sometimes we'll cross the line into self-sabotage by inviting critiques to arrive early. Unsure whether we're on the right track with our project, we can easily fall into the trap of asking someone to give their opinion on our work-in-progress. Doing this is harmful simply because the work is NOT DONE! People, even friendly ones, will naturally notice the rough spots and miss the diamonds that will emerge with polishing. Creative projects often start out as ugly ducklings; when we allow people to critique them too early, their comments may dishearten us into scrapping our work before it has a chance to grow into its true beauty. "But it would be nice to get a *little* feedback," we may say. We can get feedback, but we must do it very carefully, lest we allow criticism to make us feel the pain of shame.

> *A successful person is one who can lay a firm foundation with the bricks that others throw at him or her.*
>
> -David Brinkley

CRITICISM AND SHAME

When we throw the brakes onto our creative projects before we have a chance to act on our ideas, it's often because we fear the feelings of shame that criticism can evoke. Shame is a tool that people use to control others, somewhat like a torture device. As kids, when we acted outside adults' expectations, we heard, "Shame on you!" AKA "Your actions are embarrassing to me, so I will respond by making you feel worthless." The feeling of shame is entirely unpleasant, so it's common ammunition people use when our self-expression pulls them outside their comfort zones. Bursts of unapologetic creative expression frighten some people, and they fight back by pushing our shame buttons.

Because it's our true selves who create, our creations tell the truth—about ourselves, about what we think, about how we feel. Sometimes the truth is unvarnished and raw, not socially acceptable. The truth can be disconcerting; that's why it often feels more comfortable to tell a little white lie than to speak honestly. Creative expression does not lie, nor does it beat around the bush. Just as we may have been made to feel ashamed as kids for telling uncomfortable truths like, "Ms. Jones, your socks don't match!" we may be made to feel ashamed for speaking honestly through our creative work.

One of the chief vehicles for shame is criticism. While not all criticism aims to shame, critiques that are shaming can wreak havoc on our creative health. When we encounter nasty critics who try to shame us for doing our thing, it's vital that we recognize the shame and work to release it from our minds. If left untreated, shame can grow like cancer, infecting our self-confidence, undermining our sense of identity, and even tainting the act of creating itself. Fear of shame is why insightful employees keep quiet at meetings, or why incredibly funny people refuse to get on stage at the comedy club. We can rid ourselves of shame by learning more about criticism, and refusing to accept critiques that seek to shame us.

TWO TYPES OF CRITICISM AND HOW TO DEAL WITH THEM

There are two general types of criticism: the helpful kind and the unhelpful kind. Helpful criticism is valuable; it teaches us something. If we receive a music judge's sheet that says, "All notes above F are sharp; check intonation," reading it may feel rotten, but the judge's feedback gives us valuable information that can help us grow as musicians. Helpful criticism tends to lead to realizations: "OH, so THAT'S what was wrong. Now I can fix it!" Unhelpful criticism, on the other hand, ridicules us and makes us feel awful, but does little else. This type of criticism is heavy on venom but light on details; often, it's difficult to deal with simply because it's so ambiguous. Harsh, vague critiques like "Why are you even singing?"

or "Your writing stinks," do nothing but break us down. While we can't control the criticism we'll encounter, one of the kindest things we can do for ourselves is to define which types of criticism are helpful and which aren't worth our time.

Although receiving criticism rarely is an enjoyable experience, some criticism is appropriate, valid, and helpful. For example, if our guitar teacher observes that our rhythm sounds shaky and suggests some exercises to practice, her critique can help us become better guitarists by revealing our weak spots and showing us how to fix them. However, because criticism generally doesn't feel good, it can be difficult to discern which critiques are legitimate and which are not. Here are some qualities that helpful criticism generally has:

> **It comes from someone who isn't an Artist-in-Hiding**
> **It is specific and detailed.**
> **It has a basis in fact, not just opinion.**
> **It comes with specific suggestions for improvement.**
> **It is not shaming, insulting, or derogatory.**
> **It is usually something we consent to hearing.**
> **It doesn't indicate trash on the critic's side of the street.**

Receiving helpful criticism is easier when we approach it with an open mind. As adults, it can be incredibly difficult to be called out on our mistakes; after all, we're leaders at home, at work, and in society. Our first reaction to our guitar teacher's comment might be to snap, "I KNOW!" But if we make the effort to slow down, open our minds, carefully listen to the critique, and see what we can take from it, we may find that we can use it to move us toward our creative goals. If possible, asking questions of our critics can show us where to improve, or let us know if the criticism is even valid. If we respond to our teacher by asking, "Where exactly is it off?" or "What can I do to fix it?" we open the door to new learning experiences that can help us build our creative skills and techniques.

Just as helpful criticism has qualities we can look for, there are also hallmarks of unhelpful criticism that can help us detect and avoid it. Here are some signs that indicate unhelpful criticism:

> **It comes from an inexperienced person or an Artist-in-Hiding.**
>
> **It's vague; it says you stink but doesn't tell why.**
>
> **It is rooted entirely in opinion; it can't be backed up by facts.**
>
> **It focuses on you as a person, not on your work.**
>
> **It offers no specific suggestions for improvement.**
>
> **It's shaming and derogatory, makes you want to cry or quit.**
>
> **It seems like the critic's side of the street is a total wreck!**

When we are the unfortunate recipients of unfair, unhelpful criticism, we have an important job to do: to give our Inner Artist extra care and protection. To our Artist, unhelpful criticism is comparable to assault—she is injured, bruised, shaken, and afraid. When our little Artist is attacked, it's easy for her to become withdrawn and volatile, skittish and mistrustful like an abused animal. Although we may want to stuff our feelings and pretend like we're OK, it is our duty to acknowledge the pain of receiving unhelpful criticism, and to take time to comfort our Artist and ourselves. We must use our tools, like saying affirmations like there's no tomorrow, looking out for self-doubt, and sharing our feelings with trusted friends. Above all, we can't let nasty critics win. We MUST continue to show up and create, and to nurture ourselves and our ideas.

FIVE CRITICISM-BLASTING TECHNIQUES

Critiques, especially the unhelpful kind, may replay in our minds long after the hall is empty and our critics have gone home. Here are five simple mindset shifts that can bring us comfort after we've been harshly criticized.

1. Walk a Mile in My Shoes - Being an armchair general is easy to do; remember, humans don't have to be coached to criticize. Unfortunately, we'll sometimes be targets of reviewers who are mean just to be mean. However, when we encounter one of these nasty critics, we may find solace in asking, "Could this critic actually do what I do?" Nine times out of ten, the answer will be no! Often we can tell just by reading a review whether the critic is a true practitioner of an art form, or whether they're just a vitriolic armchair general. If we look carefully, we may notice another common malady in critics—that they themselves are Artists-in-Hiding. Jealousy that you're out there and they're stuck in their hiding places can make their reviews particularly acidic.

2. Criticism as a Badge of Honor - Criticism is an honor bestowed upon people who are out there doing things and taking risks. We're taking action instead of letting life pass us by. Whenever you go out and do what you love, there will be folks watching from the sidelines. Some will cheer, and some will fuss, but either way, they're sitting there watching *you*. By simply following your dreams and being yourself, you've attracted an audience! And no matter what they say, having a following is pretty cool!

3. Keep Your Eye on the Ball - Imagine you're a quarterback at the Super Bowl. There's a huge stadium of people surrounding you, all making noise. Some are booing, some are cheering, and some are just having a drunken good time. There are TV cameras everywhere and you know that millions of people across the country are scrutinizing you, critiquing you. It can be easy to focus on the fans or the cameras, but to win you must focus on one thing and one thing only: the game. Likewise, to succeed creatively, we must focus on our work. We train ourselves not to seek validation in others' opinions, but in our work itself. When we keep our focus on what we do, we win.

4. Return to Sender - Once, when the Buddha was speaking, a man interrupted him with a flood of criticism. Buddha waited until the man stopped and asked, "If a person offered a gift to another but the gift was declined, to whom would the gift belong?" The man answered, "To the one who offered it." "Then," replied Buddha, "I decline to accept your criticism and ask that you keep it for yourself!" We can choose to be like the wise Buddha, and simply decide not to accept the "gift" of criticism.

5. Criticism Reflects on the Critic - Instead of worrying what people say about us when they criticize, it can be helpful to think about what people's criticisms say about *them*. If someone attacks us with scathing criticism, often the assault isn't about us at all. The critic may be venting over something totally unrelated to us. Or, they may have an overwhelming desire to show people that they're right. Sometimes, the critic may just be having a bad day. Whatever the reason, it's freeing to realize that many critiques we receive don't reflect on us at all!

Procrastination

Another stumbling block that can trip us up on the creative path is procrastination. Procrastination takes many forms: acting like a workaholic, creating unnecessary busyness in our lives, and even just being lazy. Whatever form procrastination takes, it's a huge block that stands between us and our creative projects.

It's common to repeatedly delay our creative projects because of fear. Creating requires that we be true to ourselves, that we express how we really feel, and that we have FUN. For many of us, allowing ourselves to do these things isn't easy. We know that creating can open a vault of intense emotions and uncomfortable truths that we'll need to deal with. We know that when we're happily working on a project, it's a great opportunity for Naysayers, Needies, and Guilt-trippers to whine that we're not paying enough attention to them. Creating also carries some form of risk; our project may open us up to criticism, or it may turn out badly. On the other hand, it may turn out extremely well and the world's attention will suddenly focus on us, making our lives very different than they are now. There are many "what ifs" to consider, but the problem is, considering these possibilities often leads to fear. And fear often leads us to sit on our hands and do nothing!

Procrastination manifests itself in many ways, but all of them have one thing in common: excuses, excuses, excuses. If we tend to procrastinate by burying ourselves in other, less creative work, our excuse might be, "But I'm working! I have deadlines to meet!" On the other hand, if we tend to generate unnecessary clutter and busyness in our lives to avoid starting our projects, we may find ourselves saying, "I'll get creative after I do the dishes. But maybe I should clean the tub, too. And then maybe the garage as well..."

A great way to knock out excuses is to establish regular creative habits. If we practice good habits like writing in our journal each day, giving ourselves regular Creative Time, and looking for the Helping Hand in our lives, we set up routines that make creating easier and sap the power of our excuses. When we think of the lives of creative people, many of us assume that each day is a wild, unscheduled free-for-all. Not so! Creative people with concrete goals and daily habits that reinforce those goals are the ones who blast through excuses and achieve their creative dreams.

Procrastination can also be pushed aside with a little help from our creative friends. Our friends support us, give us safe outlets to share our feelings and ideas, and most importantly, they can bug us if we become lazy! When a friend asks us how our project is going, mentions that they're excited to see the finished product, or hints that it's been a while since we've mentioned our painting, they remind us to persevere on our creative journey instead of allowing life to push our ideas aside. When we're looking for friends to help us stay on course, it's helpful to find folks who are walking the creative path as well. A friend who is also on a creative journey can help us much more than someone who doesn't quite understand what we're doing. A good rule of thumb is to look for "wake up call" buddies behind our Purple Velvet Rope. If they're supportive enough to be allowed behind the rope, they'll likely be supportive enough to keep us on our creative toes.

> *I don't wait for moods. You accomplish nothing if you do that. Your mind must know it has got to get down to work.*
>
> *-Pearl S. Buck*

Taking the Leap

It's easy to sit and think about creativity, talk about creativity, and theorize about creativity. While all these activities are helpful, the only way to truly unleash our creativity is to create! To turn our dreams into reality, we must gather all the lessons we've learned and take action!

RISKY BEHAVIOR IS A GOOD THING

With action comes risk, and taking healthy risks is good for creative people. Taking creative risks pushes us out of our comfort zones and forces us to learn new things. Although we may feel uncomfortable, taking the risk of trying something new strengthens us and leads us to new discoveries. As we push past our perceived limits, our new creative activities gradually become easier, more fluid, more natural, until we realize that our comfort zone has expanded and we're once again standing inside it!

In many situations, taking risks does not ensure success. Gambling our life savings in a poker game or jumping off the roof are both risks, but the results are almost guaranteed to be disastrous. However, when we take the leap and write the first paragraph of that book we've always wanted to write, we're taking a risk that's a win-win all around. When we take creative risks, we challenge ourselves to stretch our abilities and grow both as creators and as people. Facing a challenge head-on, like Attack Velvet does, bolsters our self-confidence and makes meeting the next challenge that much easier. When we become willing to take the risk of starting a project, we create the opportunity for a new part of our life to flourish. When we write our first few clunky choruses, we open the possibility of developing a fulfilling songwriting practice. When we sew our first crooked pair of blue jeans, it becomes possible to keep practicing until we're excellent clothing designers. By beginning, we set the wheels of progress into motion.

WE MUST SOUND BAD TO SOUND GOOD

When we embark on a creative endeavor, many of us wish for instant success. Success feels good, and brings positive recognition from others. But in reality, much of the success involved in our first projects will be the fact that we did them at all. Often, our early creative efforts will be straight up BAD...and that's OK!

When we're learning, mistakes are the norm. They're inevitable and necessary. To learn to play the right notes, we must experience what it feels like to play them wrong. To figure out how to raise our clay pot higher, we need to flop a few times until we determine how fast the wheel should turn and how our hands should move. There is no shame in making mistakes, because mistakes beckon progress. When we look at our first rotten painting, read over our first thumbs-down screenplay, drink from our first lopsided teacup, we are observing the beginning of a lifetime of ever more beautiful works of art. A great way to bypass our desire for instant success is to set out to create something that's *simply awful*. When our goal is to make bad art, the pressure to be perfect is relieved, allowing us to create happily. We celebrate our projects, no matter how awful they are, and then make another, and another. This is *practice*, and practice is the force that pushes us forward on the creative path. In time, practice turns ugly ducklings into lovely swans.

Learning the Discipline

Even before we set out on the creative path, many of us have a specific artistic medium we want to practice: music, painting, dance, acting, the list goes on and on. However, every mode of creative communication has one thing in common—you can't learn it overnight. Despite the fact that the arts are open and imaginative by nature, each discipline has skills, techniques, theory, and history that we must understand to participate fully. Just as we practiced shifting our mindsets toward the positive side early in our creative journey, we must practice once again as we strengthen our artistic abilities and understanding.

It's an unfortunate fact, but I've heard people say, "I don't want to learn more about my art form because it'll stifle my creativity." How tragic! This is like telling your lover that you don't want to talk to him because it'll "ruin the magic." The very best creators are lifelong learners, hungry for new insights about their medium of choice, excited to learn more about the subject they love most. Just as couples who stay happily married for decades write each other love letters and share the details of their lives together each day, creative people who truly enjoy their work relish time spent deepening their artistic understanding. Successful creative people understand that knowledge and creativity are far from being mutually exclusive.

Music quite possibly has the most rules of any creative discipline: Rules about timing, harmony, intonation, composition, transposition, fingering, breathing, bowing, tone. Nonetheless, it is relatively easy to approach the learning of all these elements with a spirit of life and creativity. In fact, it can be said that creativity is vital to practicing. When a young musician gets stuck on a measure she can't figure out, she has two choices: quit, or devise (create) a way to work on that measure to get it right. Trying to memorize scales by rote can take weeks, but learning a scale by improvising on it, creating something unique with the notes, can produce results in MINUTES.

The same spirit of open exploration applies in all disciplines: "What would the flower petal look like if I moved my brush like this?" "If I relax my back, can I drop a little further into my plié?" When we consciously look for ways to incorporate creativity into our learning of technique, our skills become infused with energy and vitality—and our creative side gains more possibilities to play with as we master new techniques.

> *The possession of knowledge does not kill the sense of wonder and mystery. There is always more mystery.*
>
> *-Anaïs Nin*

GET YOURSELF A FABULOUS TEACHER

When we teach ourselves, we tend to end up reinventing the wheel. We don't have anyone accompanying us on our journey and sharing the tips that can help us work with fluency and ease. But when we find a teacher, we gain a direct connection to the wealth of understanding that an experienced practitioner of our art form has developed. For those of us who want to learn about a specific creative discipline, finding a teacher is an investment in ourselves that can lead us to exciting discoveries for years to come.

Thanks to technology, museums, and libraries, we can also easily learn from the masters of every art form, both living and deceased, both here and abroad. We can saturate our ears with jazz for little monetary investment. We can watch the heavyweights of dance, music, and theatre perform for free on YouTube. We have access to endless information about creative disciplines of all kinds. Studying up on our art of choice doesn't have to be drudgery; it can be an exhilarating exploration. There's not much I enjoy more than spending an afternoon with an enormous stack of research on music and the brain. I sit and read and take notes; I don't make a sound, but nevertheless I leave the library on a high of musical excitement from learning new things about my art form.

As long as we don't fall into the trap of putting our teachers or the fellow creators we learn about on pedestals, we can research and discover to our heart's content. If we practice a certain art form, it's entirely possible that during the course of our lifelong creative journey, we'll be able to function at the same level as many of the masters we read about. Even if we just want to lead more interesting and creative lives, it's entirely possible for us to become the happiest and most imaginative people we know. And all that's required right now is to paint that first stroke, to crack that first book, to find that first cool video, to simply BEGIN.

Creative Homework

1. Criticism - What are some of your fears about criticism? Think about some times in your past when you've experienced helpful criticism as well as unhelpful criticism. How did each make you feel? Think of times when you've been able to learn from criticism you've received. How did you find the lesson within the critique?

2. The Procrastination Game - This week, see how many ways you can find yourself procrastinating about being creative. Make note of all the excuses you come up with, and notice if they have a theme. Are you burying yourself in uncreative work? Stirring up drama to avoid your art? Just being lazy? Can you create some ways to disarm these excuses?

3. Worst-Case/Best-Case - Think of the absolute worst thing that could happen if you started a creative project. Be imaginative and vivid; feel free to make the apocalypse look like child's play. Now, turn it around. What are some good things that might come out of starting your project? Are there more bad things to be had, or more good things?

***4. Begin. - This week, your #1 job is to go home and start working on a creative project. Pick one of the ideas you listed last week in your Creative Homework, and start working on it. You may hear a variety of excuses pop up, all kinds of anxious warnings from the Critic to stay in your comfort zone, and all manner of worries that everyone's going to make fun of what you've done. Deal with them in any way that's effective for you, and just start. Remember, our first creation is rarely our finest. So create something horrid this week, and enjoy every minute of it!

5. Good Habits Checkpoint - Did you cultivate good creative habits this week? What are some of the creative activities you did?

Chapter 7
Sights along the Creative Path

Goal: To gain a greater understanding of the creative process and discover some common happenings on the creative journey.

Discovering the Creative Process

Now that we've learned how to begin our creative projects, many of us may be wondering, "Now what?" We may feel confused about what to do next or unsure if our projects are headed in the right direction. At this point in our development, we can benefit greatly from studying models of the creative process. Developed by researchers who have devoted their lives to studying creativity, the three models we'll present here can help us understand how our projects may unfold in our lives. As you read, reflect on how these models resonate with your own creative experience, and use them to start building your own understanding of the creative process.

THE WALLAS STAGE MODEL

Presented in 1926 by Graham Wallas in his book *The Art of Thought*, the Wallas Stage Model explains the creative process in a series of five stages:

1. Preparation
We gather expertise and explore the details of a problem. Preparation can include all our previous education and experiences that brought us to the point of working on a particular project.

2. Incubation
The problem recedes into the subconscious mind and nothing seems to be happening.
(In reality, our minds are processing ideas!)

3. Intimation
We get a feeling that a solution is on its way.

4. Illumination/Insight
A creative idea bursts into our consciousness.

5. Verification
We take the raw material of our idea and consciously evaluate, adjust, and apply it.

To illustrate how Wallas' model might unfold in your life, I'll share an example from mine: the Sock-A-Thon song! In late 2008, I was commissioned to write the theme song for a Sock-A-Thon to raise money for the homeless. I began by exploring possibilities, drawing from the information I had about the Sock-A-Thon, as well as from the knowledge I'd gained from years of musical study. I investigated my potential song from many angles—ruminating on different styles, lyrics, and chord progressions—until I was so tired of thinking about the song that I *had* to put it away and focus on other things. A few days later, I was startled out of bed in the wee hours of the morning with a driving techno beat and some words, "What do we do when the news is bad?" My song was coming in the night, *demanding* to be realized! I jumped out of bed, grabbed my recorder, and sang what I was hearing; and thus, a song was born. Later, when I was more awake, I went back and verified my ideas; I revised the lyrics, tweaked the rhythms, and polished my work into a nice recording that drew rave reviews from the sock people!

While Wallas' stages are alive and well in artistic pursuits like songwriting, the model isn't limited to use in the arts. In outlining his stages, Wallas describes preachers, lawyers, mathematicians, and scientists moving through the stages as they created sermons, closing arguments, and theories. In fact, Wallas' model was inspired by the work of a German physicist, Hermann von Hemholtz, who introduced the ideas of Preparation, Incubation, and Illumination as routes to scientific discovery. By drawing from such a wide range of disciplines, Wallas reminds us that practitioners of the fine arts aren't the only people who are creative. When we use our unique understanding to devise, evaluate, and implement new ideas, we are all artists, no matter what our job titles may be.

Although the Wallas model describes an exciting process that creators from a variety of disciplines can experience, it has been criticized for relying so heavily on unexplainable subconscious activity to describe the creative process. The fact that much of the model's action happens beyond our consciousness suggests that the creative process is something we can't fully control, and reinforces the myth that we must be touched by some mysterious "muse" to create. Our next model addresses this issue by describing the creative process as a sequence of conscious thoughts and actions.

OSBORN'S MODEL FOR CREATIVE THINKING

Alex Osborn, the creator of brainstorming, embraced a seven-step model of the creative process that combines both imaginative and analytical thinking.

> **1. Orientation** - Pointing up the problem
>
> **2. Preparation** - Gathering pertinent data
>
> **3. Analysis** - Breaking down the relevant material
>
> **4. Ideation** - Piling up alternatives by way of ideas
>
> **5. Incubation** - Letting up, to invite illumination
>
> **6. Synthesis** - Putting the pieces together
>
> **7. Evaluation** - Judging the resulting ideas

Although Osborn's model is similar to Wallas' model in some ways, it's unique because it highlights the importance of analytical thought in the creative process. Osborn shows us that creating isn't a strictly imaginative endeavor; our creativity is enriched when we use analytical thinking to define a problem and build a framework for solving it. We don't just come up with a problem and then allow the subconscious mind to take over; rather, we dig into our project, ask questions, and explore every detail we can. This conscious critical thinking sparks our imaginative abilities, which in turn allow us to pile up ideas that can help us solve our problem.

I'll take you through Osborn's model using my current project, this book! I began a couple of years ago with a big, general problem: "I'm tired of hearing people dismissing their creativity, and I want to DO something about it!" This issue had plenty of passion behind it, but in order to create a workable solution, I had to point up the problem by making it clear and specific. To do this, I asked questions: "Who dismisses their creativity the most? Why? What do they say? How can I reach them?" When my problem had become clear and I knew I wanted to solve it by writing a book, I started gathering data: reading books and articles about creativity, attending women's empowerment seminars, and talking to scores of women about talent, art, and imagination. As I researched, I began to notice certain themes emerging again and again; these themes became a framework that kept me organized through the rest of the process.

Upon my framework, I piled ideas. Many of these ideas came as a result of answering my own questions: "What if I tried this?" or "How can I say that?" Other times, I formed ideas by practicing healthy creative habits like writing in my journal. Because I had built a framework, in the form of a general chapter outline, I had a place to store all my ideas as they came. If I got an idea about the creative process, I typed it into Chapter Seven. Something about fear? That landed in Chapter Three. In this stage, I didn't revise anything; I just poured any and every idea onto the page. My college English teacher Professor Eadus called this "puking," dumping ideas onto the page with reckless abandon (and without judgment). In this sense, I "puked" throughout the writing of this book! ☺

Although I'd used a great deal of analytical thinking and planning skills to create this book, I still was able to experience the calm of Incubation and the thrill of Illumination. Several paragraphs in this book woke me up at night, asking to be written, while others came after a lazy day at the park when the book was the last thing on my mind. In this way, Osborn's model captures the best of both worlds—we can both consciously think creatively, and enjoy the less-explainable gifts the Creative Spirit leaves in our minds.

As I write this, I'm synthesizing and evaluating. These final stages have melded together; they repeat and reinforce each other. I revise a paragraph and then evaluate how it sounds. I come up with an exercise and test it out with my creativity group. I'll continue practicing these last two stages on my book for quite some time as I prepare it for publication, and even further down the road when it's time to release a new edition or write a new book entirely. And then, the process will begin once again!

FRITZ'S PROCESS FOR CREATION

In his 1991 book *Creating*, Robert Fritz describes the creative process as an eight-part sequence that's not unlike the blues form in music. He presents his model as a way to focus our creative work, much like the chord changes in the blues shape a musician's solo. Just as a musician can play many melodies over the same chord changes, Fritz asserts we can create a wide variety of things—from art to dinner parties—using the same model of the creative process.

1. Conception - We form an idea of what we want to create.

2. Vision - We build a detailed vision of our desired result.

3. Current reality - We describe what we currently have in relation to what we want. The discrepancy between our Current Reality and Vision creates tension that propels our work forward.

4. Take action - We take the steps necessary to reach our Vision.

5. Adjust, learn, evaluate, adjust - We learn from what we've done and adjust our approach as needed.

6. Building momentum - As we accomplish small goals on the way toward our Vision, we add new energy to our work.

7. Completion - We finish, and declare that our creation is done!

8. Living with your creation - We accept our creation and allow it to stand on its own. Our relationship to our creation changes; now we aren't just creators, we're audience members as well.

While Osborn's model involves a great deal of thinking, Fritz's model centers on *doing*. If we tend to procrastinate or overplan our creative projects, following Fritz's action-packed model may propel us toward meeting our goals. In Fritz's model, we don't think for thinking's sake; we use thinking as a tool to hone our understanding of our Current Reality and Vision, and to evaluate our progress. We gather creative momentum not by sitting and planning, but by doing, learning, and actively working toward our goal.

In addition to being action-oriented, Fritz's model lends structure to our projects by asking us to identify in detail the results we want and the place we're starting. Rather than trying to pile up many possible ideas, we focus our efforts by aiming for one specific result, or Vision. If our Vision is a tasty vegetarian dinner, we can infer that a trip to the butcher shop won't be part of our creative process! When we combine this knowledge of our Vision with an understanding of our starting point, or Current Reality, we uncover details that can show us exactly what to do next. If we realize our starting point for the vegetarian dinner is a freezer full of ground beef, we know that our next step must be a trip to the produce aisle! When we fully understand what we're doing, we give our projects direction. With its focus on learning the details, Fritz's model helps us develop specific actions that move our projects forward.

While Fritz's entire model is helpful, I chose to share it mainly because of the final two steps, *Completion* and *Living with your creation*. While our other models provide excellent ways to understand the creative process, neither openly acknowledges the importance of a project's ending. Many of us find it hard to stop revising our work, leaving our projects forever unfinished. Others of us may be able to finish, but may resist sharing our completed projects with others. When we don't allow our projects to become finished, we end up in a frustrating hamster wheel of revision, running ourselves ragged with perfectionism. Likewise, when we complete a project but hide it from the world, we prevent others (and ourselves) from enjoying and gaining insight from our work. Learning to accept our work can be tough, but it's necessary for creative success. Creating is a form of communication, a way to share our personal truth with the rest of humankind. It's only when we learn to accept our work that we can release it to touch other people's lives.

WHAT THESE MODELS HAVE IN COMMON

Each of our models is unique; after all, they were devised by different people decades apart from one another. However, as people on a creative quest, we can gain valuable insight about the creative process by comparing what these models have in common:

> **Each of these models asks us to actively learn and pay attention.**
>
> **The creative process uses both imaginative & analytical thinking.**
>
> **Creating requires action; getting ideas is only part of the process.**
>
> **Most of these models suggest that down time helps foster ideas.**

For us creative people, these commonalities show us that:

> **Making efforts to learn about and better understand our projects enriches our creative process.**
>
> **We must set aside the belief that people in disciplines outside the arts aren't creative. Much of the creative process involves critical thinking, which is prized in many subjects.**
>
> **We must stimulate our brains often, cultivating our abilities to think both rationally and imaginatively.**
>
> **Being creative isn't simply churning out ideas; it's taking action to turn them into reality.**
>
> **We must allow ourselves processing time when we create. Down time and reflection are vital parts of the creative process.**

In our everyday lives, we may hear a number of misleading ideas about the creative process, and often, this misinformation is disempowering and limiting. However, when we study these and other models of the creative process, we infuse our understanding with the work of people who are committed to uncovering the truth about creativity. As you continue on your journey, I encourage you to keep learning and developing your own understanding of the creative process. When we take time to study the creative process, we gain insights that can help shape our future creative experiences.

Scenery on the Creative Path

On every voyage, there are sights to see and challenges to face along the way, and the creative journey is no exception. As we walk the creative path, we'll encounter a wide variety of terrain. Sometimes our ideas dry up and we feel like we're stuck in an arid, endless desert. Other times we feel like we're bobbing in an ocean of inspiration, surrounded by so many ideas that we can't keep track of them all. Still other times we're climbing mountains, slowly finishing momentous projects and meeting audacious goals. In this section, we'll begin learning how to navigate several common landscapes we'll encounter on the creative path.

DESERTS AND OCEANS

At times during our journey, we may find ourselves walking through deserts, stretches of the path when we feel like our ideas have completely run dry. Deserts feel quiet but not peaceful, still but not serene. We may sense that something great is coming over the horizon, but all we can see at the moment is sand, sand, sand. We grow impatient with the fruitless dunes around us, and become thirsty for good ideas. We cross creative deserts for a variety of reasons: maybe we've unknowingly fallen into a creative rut, or we've just finished something big and are in need of rest. Possibly, our ideas are just stewing in Wallas' Incubation stage for an extended period of time. Whatever the cause, deserts can feel hot, dry, and unlivable; after all, creative people enjoy new ideas, and in deserts, there are not many to be had.

Oceans, on the other hand, are times on the journey when we feel absolutely flooded with possibilities. We're adrift in inspiration, surrounded by an ever-deepening sea of ideas, breathing air that's misty with potential—and we're completely overwhelmed. We may feel like we'll never get everything done that we need to do, or like opportunities keep slipping through our already busy fingers. In times like these, we may be tempted to become a "jack of all trades, master of none" with our creative projects. We might start an exciting project and then put it aside to work on another, and another. Creative oceans can be exciting, but can easily swallow our time, energy, and focus.

When we're flooded out or dried up, we may feel so off-kilter that we consider abandoning the creative path and returning to life as we knew it before we found our creativity. We may worry that it's our fault we're stuck in a desert or ocean, and begin doubting our skills: "If I were *really* creative, this wouldn't be happening!" We can fight this self-doubt with a dose of reality. Creative deserts and oceans aren't signs of artistic sickness; rather, they're as normal as real deserts and oceans are in the natural world. They're merely landscapes, and like the landscapes that decorate our planet, they don't go on forever. Every desert eventually gives way to greener pastures, and every ocean touches the shore. Although pushing through these extreme terrains can be difficult, as long as we keep going, we'll reach the other side.

Perhaps one of the best things to do in ocean times is to pour our ideas into our journals, and return in desert times to read what we've written. When we feel like we're drowning in a sea of inspiration, we capture as many ideas as we can in the pages of our journals. Then, when we're sitting in the lonely desert, our journals can bring us cheer—and even spring up a river of possibility right in the middle of the desolate sands!

MOUNTAINS: ACHIEVING OUR CREATIVE GOALS

Mountains on the creative path are our journeys toward achieving our goals, the creative process that turns ideas into reality. When we get a great idea and decide to bring it to fruition—writing a book, working up a concerto, painting a mural—our climb begins. Creative mountains can be both exhilarating and trying. We experience the joy of realizing our ideas, but also face the challenges of solving problems, staying focused, and overcoming fear. When we climb creative mountains, we put our understanding into action to make our dreams come true.

Creative mountain climbing is usually a long-term endeavor, as our projects may require weeks, months, or years to complete. On such an extended journey, we must make the effort to keep ourselves happy and motivated to continue. We nurture our creativity by writing in our journals, hanging out with creative friends, and taking regular Creative Time. Although we're working toward a goal, we make sure to listen to our Inner Artist and approach our work in a light and playful manner. When climbing feels like a chore, we give ourselves a break. When we're hungry and tired, we eat and sleep. When we treat ourselves well, our climb toward our goals is joyful, satisfying work.

For many of us, the last few feet of the mountain are the most arduous to climb. The possibility of finishing a project often sparks fears that can intimidate us into turning back before we reach the top. As Fritz's model reminds us, the final step of the creative process is living with what we've made; however, many of us fear the change that a finished project might bring to our lives. We may have the peak in our sights, the end just a few strokes away, but fear makes us retreat. We must push through our fear, simply because the pain of abandoned projects can be unbearable. For creative people, abandoning a project can feel like deserting a child; we feel regret, anger, and grief over the treasure we've left behind. Although the final steps may be tough, we usually find that it's easier to finish our climb than to stage a fearful retreat.

On the other hand, some of us may have trouble knowing when to *stop* climbing. We may worry that as the top draws nearer, so does the possibility of criticism. We imagine the audience's response, and it scares us into inviting a new wave of perfectionism to wash over our work. Driven by perfectionism, we overclimb, scrutinizing and revising in an anxious effort to make our work "good enough." As we approach the peak, we must pay attention to where our project leads us and where it wants to end. If we step past the point where our work feels done to make it "just a little bit better," we fall.

Although climbing creative mountains is challenging, the skills we've learned throughout our course can help us bring our ideas to fruition. If fear or uncertainty creep in, we can visit Chapter Three and remind ourselves how to deal with these feelings in a positive way. We can steady our feet by staying in the moment and listening to what our Inner Artist and Creative Spirit are telling us. It's not uncommon for our projects themselves to show us what to do next; sometimes, projects will even tell us when they're done! All we need to do is open our minds to listen, and keep walking the path.

OUR FRIEND, FAILURE

In our creative travels, we'll inevitably cross paths with failure—a true, albeit misunderstood, friend. Many of us have been taught that failure is shameful, painful, and bad, an enemy that we want to avoid at all costs. In the realm of creativity, however, failure is a valuable ally. Failure, like anger, rarely feels good; nevertheless, it's a tool that points us in a very specific direction. We can use failure as a compass, guiding us to reflect, rethink, and retry. Success lies in our answers to the questions that failure asks us.

Although failure has never won an award for educational excellence, it is probably one of the best teachers we'll ever have. It shows us the results we get when we do the actions we did, and invites us to intelligently review our work and revise our approach. We can learn to stop fearing failure by realizing that it's a natural part of the creative process, and a normal occurrence in the lives of successful creative people. Perhaps the strongest bond that the most accomplished creators throughout history share is their willingness to accept and learn from their failures. In embracing our failures, we enable ourselves to generate new ideas that push us toward progress. Here are some ways to turn failure into a productive spark:

1. Change your views on failure and success. Failure is not a mark of weakness or inability; rather, it's a sign that you're out there *doing* something. Failing is a natural byproduct of taking healthy risks, honing your skills, and expressing your creative ideas. The act of stepping up, taking a risk, and falling short is a much better achievement than being an expert at doing nothing.

2. Keep your*self* out of it. There's a huge difference between saying, "I failed," and "I'm a failure." When we fail, it's important to recognize that although we didn't triumph this time, it doesn't mean we're incapable of succeeding. Labeling ourselves as failures shackles us with hopelessness, making us unable to move on and accomplish new things. However, if we view our *project* or *approach* as the failure, we free ourselves to try, try again!

3. Look for the lesson. Remember, failure is an excellent teacher. When we reflect on why we failed, we often discover new ideas that bring us closer to success. Thomas Edison failed about 10,000 times before he got his lightbulb to work. Instead of quitting, he used data from his failures to adjust his approach. By using failure as a positive tool, Edison enabled himself to create something that changed the world!

4. Keep on keeping on. Failure doesn't just happen once; it's an experience we'll have again and again. If we follow Edison's example and try again, we become stronger, more knowledgeable, and closer to success each time we fail.

People on the Path

Popular myths tell us that the creative life is lonely, but as we'll discover, the creative path is bustling with potential friends, allies, and colleagues. Throughout our journey, we'll have chances to build lasting friendships and fruitful collaborations with like-minded people, and chances to learn from others who are different from us. Here, we present a brief guide to interacting with fellow creators on the trail.

LEARNING TO WORK TOGETHER

One of the first things we'll learn on our journey is that creative people dig other creative people. Creative folks tend to enjoy each other's company, simply because we share an understanding and connection that we can't find with people who haven't embraced their creativity. Since we're new to the creative path, this kind of acceptance may seem foreign to us. Fortunately, we'll discover that learning how to connect with other creative people can be an easy—and enjoyable—endeavor.

When we were Artists-in-Hiding, we may have felt jealous of people who were following their creative desires. Since we've only recently come out of hiding, we might still feel residual envy toward other creative people but not understand why. If we feel this way, we can gently remind ourselves that we need not be jealous; after all, we can create, too! Although our creativity may be different from others', it is just as valid and as rich as anyone else's. On the other hand, if we encounter someone who seems creative, but who acts jealous or standoffish around other creators, it's perfectly fine to keep our distance. No matter how creative a person may seem, mean-spirited jealousy is a sign of creative illness. We don't need to stick around and get sick!

Some of us may find ourselves celebrating our own creativity, but bristling when other creators enter our space. We may fear being outshined, or enjoy our title as Resident Creative Chick and not want to share it. Driven by the scarcity mentality, this anxiety brings out an ugly selfishness that keeps us from building precious friendships with fellow creative folks. When we feel scarcity worries creeping in, it may be helpful to recall the individual nature of creativity. Nobody else's creativity can detract from our own, simply because every person's creativity is one-of-a-kind. We need not insist upon being the only creative person in the room; after all, we're already the only being in the *world* with our unique creative perspective!

When we lay our old fears aside, we realize that it's possible to connect with fellow creators and combine our skills in meaningful ways. A painter and a writer might collaborate on a book with beautiful illustrations. Several musicians might team up and start a band. Much of the time, collaborations like these evolve when creative people simply take time to sit and talk. When creative people spend time together, we often begin to bubble over with ideas. It's common to meet for dinner and have a screenplay in the works before dessert arrives! Creative people are drawn to play together, and this play can cement great working relationships as well. When we open our minds to connecting with other people on our journey, we awaken the possibility of building fruitful creative partnerships.

Once in a while, we may run across a fellow creative person whom we simply don't like. Even though we aren't acting on scarcity-based jealousy, we find that something just doesn't click between us. Don't worry; this is normal! Because creating requires us to be so true to ourselves, many creators have very distinct personalities. Sometimes, a fellow creative person's personality might naturally grate on ours, and ours may frustrate them just as much. Fortunately, we don't need to be best friends with every creative person who walks through the door. Often just making a simple effort to respect our colleagues' creativity, whether we like them or not, can make our journey much more enjoyable and bring us support from a variety of fellow travelers along the path.

HEALTHY COMPETITION

Another common way we connect with fellow creative folks is through healthy competition. We're not talking about the kind of rivalry where one artist tries to sabotage another's show to get ahead; it's more like friendly, good-natured play. At open mic nights, poets and lyricists enjoy both hearing others' work and showing off their own abilities. The same goes for musicians trading solos, or breakdancers taking turns on the floor. Playful competition helps us make new friends and motivates us to polish our skills. The defining element of healthy competition is its spirit of fun and encouragement. If we miss a note, fumble our lines, or even fall off the stage, healthy competitors won't start pushing shame buttons. Healthy creators share a common understanding of the creative path's ups and downs, and can empathize with and support each other's efforts. If we feel secure and strong in our abilities, lighthearted competition with our creative friends can be like vitamins for our creative development.

Sometimes, a sense of competition will arise in the burn of envy we feel at the sight of other people's creative victories. When we first hear of others' successes, we may be tempted to sulk, "Why can't *I* do that? Poor me!" However, once we decide to discontinue our pouting and push our pride aside, we find that other people's successes can give us a healthy dose of motivation. It takes time and conscious effort to train ourselves to channel jealousy into creative motivation, but we can learn to do it, of course, with practice! Try this: every time you feel yourself becoming jealous or resentful of another's success, turn those negative feelings around just as you'd do with the Critic's insults. If you're mad that your college roommate just released a CD, flip the feeling around and ask, "Have *I* written any songs lately?" If you're tempted to talk trash about a hot new painter you read about in the paper, try instead speaking words of encouragement to yourself: "If I show up and paint today, that could be ME tomorrow!" When we celebrate other people's successes, we also celebrate the fact that WE can succeed!

THE SLIMY SWAMPS OF SEXISM & PREJUDICE

Unfortunately, not everyone we'll meet on the creative path is supportive or kind. As a female creator, I've experienced many situations in which people judge my work not on its own merits, but by my physical appearance. Sometimes this has been benign, like when I blow a lousy solo but still get wild cheers for being a little girl with a big horn. Other times, these situations have been heartbreaking, from facing humiliating questions about who I had to sleep with to be "allowed" to play with a certain band, to having payment withheld for work I've done. Although Prejudice Attacks like these aren't the norm, they happen enough (and hurt enough) to deserve a spot in print.

When we're on the receiving end of a Prejudice Attack, we're yanked from the solid ground of the creative path and tossed into smelly, slimy swampland. Prejudice thrives in the stagnant waters of ignorance, and attackers tend to do their dirty work under mossy, murky veils of secrecy. If there's ever a time to set aside the Nasty Niceness that discourages us from speaking our minds, it's when we're in the swamps of prejudice. We are ambassadors for creativity today; we can combat ignorance with facts about strong, creative women. We have boundaries today, and we can declare how we expect to be treated. When we speak up for ourselves, we lift the veil of secrecy on which prejudiced "swamp creatures" thrive.

Speaking out against prejudice can feel quite good, and over time paves the way for more women to boldly express their ideas. But Prejudice Attacks themselves can be *terribly* painful. Creating requires us know ourselves well and express ourselves honestly. When swamp creatures douse us with their ignorance and lies, the muck doesn't hit some protective mask; rather, it deals a punishing blow directly to our Inner Artist herself. Prejudice Attacks are the ultimate in unhelpful criticism—hateful wallops of shame that mock the very core of who we are, making us question our creativity...and ourselves.

Sadly, finding support in the face of prejudice can be difficult. Often, even the most understanding people in our lives won't be able to fully comprehend the pain of a Prejudice Attack. Attacks like these are generally vague and difficult to explain, and they tend to be executed with enough subtlety that even *we* can be fooled into thinking nothing happened. Many people don't want to believe that prejudice exists. As a result, it's common to share painful stories of Prejudice Attacks only to get responses like, "Are you *sure* that's what happened?" or "I can't imagine anyone saying something like that!" Listening to people who doubt the validity of our experience is as dangerous as bending an ear to a thousand Inner Critics; it undermines our confidence and implies that our senses don't work properly enough to determine whether we've been harmed or not. Pain in our hearts is definitely not "all in our heads." Although some may dismiss our experiences, we must acknowledge and process them, lest we risk staying trapped in the swamp.

When we're ambushed by prejudiced swamp creatures, it's vital that we acknowledge our pain and make the effort to heal it. When we surround ourselves and our Artist with loving care, share our feelings with understanding friends, and ask the Creative Spirit for help, we can overcome the attack and emerge stronger for it. Above all, the ultimate weapon against prejudice is to step back onto the path and keep going. When we respond to a sexist comment by showing up at our art form the very next day, we win. When we thumb our noses at bigotry by being proud, prolific, and enduring female creators, we win. When we keep placing one foot in front of the other on the path, no matter what, we find true success.

> *Remember, Ginger Rogers did everything Fred Astaire did, but she did it backwards and in high heels.*
>
> -Faith Whittlesey

Creative Homework

1. Your Creative Process - This week, we examined three models of the creative process. How do these models relate to your creative experience? Does any specific model resonate with you? This week, create your own model of the creative process. Design it to fit your own experiences and observations, and of course, name it after yourself!

2. Geography Lesson - Think back to times in your life when you may have walked through a creative desert or ocean and not even known it, like when you had a term paper due and nothing to write, or when you were trying to pick a college major and felt overwhelmed with possibilities. How did you navigate this terrain back then? How would you navigate it today? Make a list of ideas that you can use to make yourself feel nurtured and protected during funky creative times.

3. Mountain Climber's Log - Last week, you were asked to begin a creative project. This week, continue to work on your project, your "mountain" of the moment. Like a climber, keep track of how you feel on your journey this week and make note of the scenery you pass along the way. You can write this in your journal, or just make mental notes throughout the week. Do you feel perfectionism creeping in, or have you had an encounter with our friend Failure? If so, how did you respond? What is your climbing style? Do you move slowly and steadily, or climb/work in short and productive bursts?

4. Go Do Something with Your Creative Friends - We know that hanging out with our creative friends can lead us to exciting creative partnerships. This week, pick a creative friend, and go do something fun together!

5. Sexist Pig Contingency Plan - This week, devise a plan that you will use in the event that you encounter hurtful prejudice along your creative journey. What will you say to the offender? (Feel free to be, er, colorful!) More importantly, how will you care for yourself and your Artist after a Prejudice Attack? If you like, it can be fun to practice your plan on innocent stuffed animals or pillows. ☺

6. Creative Habits Checkpoint - As we approach the end of our course, has it become easier for you to practice your good creative habits? How will you maintain healthy practices like Creative Time and Journal Habit when you're finished with this book?

Chapter 8
Your Creative Journey

Goal: To begin developing habits and routines that can sustain our creativity long after we finish reading this book.

Building a Lasting Creative Practice

Throughout this book, we've focused on leaving our hiding places behind to discover new possibilities on the creative path. We've been learning about ourselves, trying new things, and expanding our comfort zones. Today, we begin building ourselves a new comfort zone, one that includes creativity, self-nurturing, and honest expression. In this chapter, we'll learn ways to integrate creativity into our everyday lives, as we prepare for the long and rewarding journey of a blissful creative life.

One More Theory – Epstein's Generativity Theory

In Chapter Seven, we explored three models of the creative process and how they relate to our own journeys. Each of these models presents a unique perspective on creating that many of us have noticed in our own creative travels—we may have experienced the subconscious creative activity that Wallas' model describes, or understand the loving acceptance of Fritz's final stage. While these models can help us describe the process we use to turn our ideas into tangible creations, none of them explain how to *live* creatively. Generativity Theory, however, focuses less on the creative process itself, and more on cultivating practices that strengthen and sustain our creativity. Introduced in 1988 by Robert Epstein, Generativity Theory gives us skills to help our creativity flourish.

Generativity Theory suggests that creativity is a predictable and organized process that can be accessed by all people. If creativity is orderly, predictable, and accessible, we can throw out those myths about the necessity of "talent" to be creative! Although popular misconceptions tell us that creativity isn't a skill that can be learned and strengthened, Generativity Theory contends that any person can take steps to enhance their creative capabilities and monitor their progress toward greater creativity. We can fortify our creative abilities by practicing simple skills—the Four Core Competencies of Creative Expression:

Epstein's Four Core Competencies:

1. **Capturing** - Preserving new ideas as they occur to you.

2. **Challenging** - Giving yourself tough problems to solve or challenging tasks to complete.

3. **Broadening** - Learning new things, especially in subjects outside your area of expertise.

4. **Surrounding** - Changing your environment so you're surrounded with diverse, interesting people and things.

By engaging in activities that beef up our Core Competencies, we can make creative expression easier and bring creativity to a more central place in our lives. In this section, we'll explore some ways that we can strengthen our creativity by practicing Epstein's Four Core Competencies in our daily lives.

CAPTURING

Ideas behave like steam—they're thick and visible when rising from the stew pot of our minds, but they dissipate and change as they float further from the stove. Capturing is simply the act of catching our ideas before they vanish, preserving them in a form that allows us to go back and review them later. Capturing techniques vary from person to person, and we can be as creative with capturing as we are with our projects! We might sing an idea for a song into our own voicemail, or draw sketches on napkins. We can carry a notebook, sketchbook, voice recorder, or even a wad of clay to catch our latest ideas. No matter what form we use to capture ideas, capturing gives us a wide assortment of potential projects and exciting perspectives to use and enjoy.

When we capture ideas, it's imperative that we do so *quickly* and *without judgment*. As tempting as it may be to start analyzing and tweaking an idea at its inception, in capturing our only objective is to record our ideas so we won't forget them. We have all the time in the world to analyze our ideas, but there's usually only a bit of time to catch them before they, like steam, change or drift away. Capturing is a flow; we pour ideas out of our heads and into the real world. Giving the Inner Critic access to a capturing session is detrimental simply because the Critic is great at blocking up flows. When we allow ourselves to judge our thoughts as they flow out of our brains, we'll find that the flow stops—and so do our ideas.

Much of the time, the ideas we pour out won't be very good; all of them will need revising, and some just won't work at all. Fortunately, in creating, as in dressmaking, it's easier to pare down than to add on. It's better to have a ton of ideas to play with, than to toss out too many right away and end up without enough to work with later. Chemist Linus Pauling illustrated this truth beautifully when he said, "The best way to have a good idea is to have lots of ideas." He's absolutely right! Ideas are creative fuel. When we have lots of ideas churning in our minds, they polish each other, sparking new ideas, better ideas, GREAT ideas.

CHALLENGING

By challenging ourselves to solve tough problems, we stimulate our brains to devise new ideas and uncover new approaches. When we present ourselves with a challenge; for example, writing a book, all the ideas we currently have about writing a book come out to play. Many of these ideas may not work on their own, but when they interact and connect, new possibilities are born. When we challenge ourselves, we not only unleash our potential to accomplish great things, we also enrich the rest of our lives by expanding our repertoire of ideas, techniques, and responses to tough situations. As we expand our repertoire, the number of new connections we can make increases, and creative thinking begins to snowball with every challenge we accept. This is the benefit of dreaming big and taking healthy risks. If we try only "safe" projects, we don't learn anything new; however, if we take on difficult tasks that stretch our limits, our creativity and capability grow each time we sit down to work.

Failure is inherent in challenging ourselves, right down to the way our brains process ideas. The very reason that new ideas begin to flood out in a challenge is because our first idea didn't work! Only when an idea or two fails do we open ourselves to look from different perspectives, form new ideas, and try fresh approaches. When we make a habit of challenging ourselves, we become more familiar with the reality of failure. We realize that failure isn't shameful or bad; rather, it's a natural occurrence in the lives of people who aim high. By being open to challenges, we can become comfortable with failure, and even begin to see it as a good thing. When we challenge ourselves, failure is the spark that brings new ideas, and success, closer.

BROADENING

Broadening is the act of learning new things and deepening our knowledge and understanding. Taking courses, reading books, joining intelligent discussions, listening to concerts, or checking out paintings in a gallery can all strengthen the knowledge we already have while expanding our understanding of the world. Learning new things exercises our minds, adds depth to our supply of ideas, and can lead us to develop novel and unexpected creative connections!

Learning doesn't have to be limited to traditional activities like taking classes or reading books; in fact, we don't have to go anywhere or purchase any special equipment to build knowledge. When we simply pay attention to the world around us and take time to reflect on our experience, we gain a wealth of understanding that can help us develop innovative ideas. Observing the backyard in great detail or savoring the subtle nuances of cooking dinner can both be powerful ways to enrich our understanding. Any effort we make to acquire new information and perspectives can boost our creativity and broaden our sense of possibility.

SURROUNDING

"Variety is the spice of life!" captures the spirit of surrounding. Surrounding means that we change our environment frequently; we hang out with a variety of people and fill our lives with interesting things. Just as learning about diverse subjects helps us make new connections, living in a stimulating environment enriches our supply of ideas and inspiration. Because different people talk about different subjects in different ways, interacting with a diverse group of people challenges our brains to work in new ways. Changing our surroundings can have a similar effect, whether we rearrange the furniture in our studio or take a nice vacation and explore a new place. Giving our brains an abundance of diverse information keeps them from getting locked into routine behaviors. When we consciously stay out of ruts, we place ourselves in the flow of ideas.

Sometimes, surrounding brings up fear and anxiety because it asks us to change. Although we know that adding variety to our lives will nourish our creativity, we may complain, "I don't want to remodel my kitchen!" or "But I'm not a people person! How am I supposed to meet all these friends?" Fortunately, we don't have to completely change our lives to be more creative—we just mix things up *a little bit*. We might start exchanging small talk with the barista each morning, or try a new recipe once a week. Even tiny changes like waking up an hour earlier or putting fresh flowers in the living room can refresh us with new ideas and energy.

GETTING INTO IT

When we try new things like building our Core Competency skills, we may encounter an initial hurdle of fear or uncertainty. We may be excited about signing up for a class to broaden our knowledge of our art form, or feel ready to take on that big, detailed project, but as the new activity approaches, we may find ourselves hitting that "Ohhhh, I don't know about this!" hurdle. Feeling anxious about the effects these changes may have on our lives, we respond by procrastinating or running the other way. But the only way to become comfortable with the creative process is to jump this hurdle and get started. When we hear our minds say, "Well, maybe I shouldn't..." when a new opportunity arises, we no longer have to run or play dead. Instead, we can ask ourselves, "What do I have to lose?" If the new activity won't kill or maim us, it might be something we'll enjoy! When we take actions that boost our Core Competencies, the only thing we have to lose is our creative blockage.

To help you discover specific ways to bring more creativity into your life, Dr. Epstein has set up a website that offers a short test to determine your strengths and needs in each competency area. Unlike many others, this test doesn't set out to determine whether you're creative or not, but instead seeks to show you what you can do to further enrich your creative abilities. Take the test at http://www.mycreativityskills.com. For further reading on ways to strengthen your skills in each competency area, check out Dr. Epstein's *Big Book of Creativity Games*.

> *All children are artists. The problem is how to remain an artist once one grows up.*
>
> -Pablo Picasso

Developing a Creative Routine

Just as doing activities to boost our Core Competencies can enhance our creativity, bringing order and regularity to our endeavors can help us sustain our creative practices over long periods of time. When we establish creative routines, we set aside special time to practice our art forms. We mark this time as sacred territory and don't allow other "stuff" to get in its way. Although popular myths suggest that creators live haphazardly, in reality, living intentionally is one of the most powerful ways to support our creativity. Building a creative routine doesn't mean we're rigid or boring; it simply means we refuse to leave our creativity to chance.

A LITTLE MORE ON SELF-DISCIPLINE FOR CREATIVE FOLKS

When we're new to the creative journey, we may be thrilled at all the novel things we're doing, excited about exploring our ideas, and hyped about getting our projects into gear. However, as we learned in Chapter Seven, some of the landscapes we'll encounter on the creative path are quite difficult to cross. We grow fatigued as we hike up seemingly endless mountains and trudge through lonely deserts. In times like these, it's easy to become enticed by the hazy glow of cop shows, gossip magazines, and other activities that are much easier to do than meeting creative challenges, and before we know it, days or weeks have passed since we've created anything! Although excitement about our work is at the core of creative achievement, sometimes we need help staying on course. A little self-discipline, in the form of practicing good creative habits, can keep us moving in the right direction.

When some of us think of discipline, we may call to mind the stoic and rigid lives of soldiers, rising at some ungodly hour, marching in the elements with a hundred pounds of equipment on their backs, following order after order. However, discipline doesn't necessarily mean punishments, rules, and deprivation; for creators, discipline involves fostering practices that help us keep our creative skills strong. Although most creative people have little use for rules, we benefit greatly from structure that supports our creative development. Our discipline is building time into each day to devote to creativity, and practicing living in the moment and paying attention. Our discipline reminds us to keep work playful, and to be true to our Inner Artist and the Creative Spirit. Our discipline asks us to show up at our projects even though they might scare us a bit, to push past our fears and do what we need to do—create. We don't practice self-discipline to make ourselves look good; we do it only to help us continue on our journey, no matter what.

Each creative person's style of getting things done is highly unique and personal. We know that the Army's form of discipline won't work well for us, because it's designed for soldiers, not creators! However, we must also realize that even ways other creative people keep themselves on track may not work for us. Some think it's best to work in the mornings, while others despise waking up early. Some get a thrill from setting goals and planning strategies to meet them, while others enjoy less structure. This is our personal journey—we don't need to force ourselves to work the way others think we should. Rather, we discipline ourselves to continue our process of self-discovery, to be true to the way we think and work, and to keep putting one foot in front of the other on the creative path. In the next section, I'll share some of the practices that have helped me develop a simple routine that nourishes and enriches my creativity. Feel free to use these as a starting point for your own practice; experiment with them, add or take away from them, but most importantly, develop a creative routine that works for you!

> *Work is either fun or drudgery. It depends on your attitude. I like fun.*
>
> -Colleen C. Barrett

YOUR CREATIVE SPACE AND TIME

As teenage girls, having our own room where we could freely express ourselves probably saved our sanity multiple times. The same holds true with our creativity. When we set up a nice place to devote entirely to creating, we establish a safe haven where we can spend time with our Inner Artist, work on our projects, and take peaceful time to think. Setting up our own creative space also has practical benefits; it gives us a place to put our instruments, paint, clay, canvas, and other creative tools. When our tools are out in plain view, creating becomes much easier, simply because there's little preparation necessary to begin our work. If our snare drum is sitting there looking at us, we're more likely to play it than if it's tucked away in the closet. When we give ourselves the gift of creative space, we build our Inner Artist a well-deserved home.

When setting up a creative space, it's important to make it your own. Decorate and furnish your space in a way that makes you feel happy and inspired, and establish guidelines with others on how you'd like your space to be treated. Your space can be a spare room in the house, a corner of your bedroom or apartment, or even a big cabinet that will hold all of your stuff. The task of finding and decorating a creative space often requires as much thought as any large project, and follows the creative process to the letter! If you'd like, setting up your space can be your first creative project.

Some of us engage in artistic disciplines that require lots of mess, noise, or special equipment. Since it's not generally feasible to weld in the living room or store our potter's wheel in the bathtub, we have to go elsewhere to do our creative work. If this is the case, we might want to focus less on the space itself and more on developing enjoyable creative rituals. When I was in music school, I wasn't able to play trombone in my thin-walled apartment, so I instead made a ritual of going to my university's music building. I would wake at 7am each day, shower, eat, and ride my skateboard to the building. I'd grab my music and climb the stairs to my favorite practice room to spend time with my trombone. I followed this routine for four years, and found so much solace in it that I didn't know what to do with myself once I graduated! Despite the fact that the trombone wasn't part of my home, it was an integral part of my life—and getting to my practice room was half the fun! Building creativity into our schedules can benefit us whether we have a regular creation location or not. The key is making creativity worthy of its own space, whether that space is on our calendars, in our homes, or both!

MOTIVATION AND PRACTICE

Having a sacred space or special routine for creating can help make showing up at our projects easier; however, no routine can guarantee that our creative engines are always purring. We're human, and sometimes we just don't feel like doing anything. We may be physically sick or tired, or we may feel too mentally scattered to engage in our work. However, in some creative disciplines especially, regular practice is vital to our success. Sometimes we simply must show up and create no matter how we feel. In this section, we'll learn more about motivating ourselves to practice even when we don't feel like it.

When I was a young musician, practice was the bane of my existence. Although I loved my trombone, sitting down to practice simply wasn't as easy as sitting down to watch television, so I never did it. In time, I realized that watching cartoons was never going to make me a better musician, and I decided to begin practicing. To my surprise, practice wasn't really that hard. The first few minutes just *felt* difficult, like the first few minutes of a workout. Engaging in the self-directed learning of practice was tricky as well, a big change from sitting and listening to teachers at school. As I practiced practicing, I developed strategies to help me push through those first few minutes and get used to being my own guide. These simple tools have helped me practice regularly for the past seventeen years:

1. The Ten Minute Rule - Often, when we don't feel like practicing, the desire is there, but we must push through an initial hurdle of lethargy to get to it. Committing to practice for a short amount of time, like ten minutes, can spark our energy enough to lead to a longer practice session. On the other hand, if we reach the ten-minute mark and don't feel like continuing, we can allow ourselves to rest and still feel proud for showing up to work.

2. Setting Goals - Perhaps the best way to make practice easier is to have a concrete goal to reach toward in every practice session. We can create large goals to achieve over time, and then break them down into smaller goals that we can accomplish in one sitting. It's much easier to "Learn the note names in measures 5-6," than it is to just "practice," simply because the former shows us exactly what we need to do.

3. Keeping a Practice Log - A practice log is a place to write down our goals and our progress toward them. Writing our goals makes us more likely to see them and less inclined to forget them. Just as having our tap shoes sitting out reminds us to dance, having our goals written down reminds us to work toward them.

4. Creating Accountability - Practicing tends to be easier when we have something to prepare for. We might set up a recital for July and spend April, May, and June getting ready, or simply tell people what we're working on so they'll ask how it's progressing. Creating deadlines or buzz gives us a tangible goal to meet, plus outside encouragement to push our efforts along.

MODERATION

While sometimes we may need motivation to begin, other times we may need help with stopping! When we're in the throes of creating, it can be incredibly difficult to get up from our work and do other things. I know this better than anyone at the moment, as I sit here at 3am feverishly typing the final pages of this book. Sure I'm drooling on the computer, but hey, I'm on a roll, I'm near the top of the peak, and I MUST KEEP WRITING! Working with this near-obsessive intensity can pull the balance right out of our lives, and isn't very healthy over extended periods of time.

Although creating is fun and engaging, working too hard and too long at our creative endeavors can lead to burnout—for both ourselves and our Inner Artist. Anyone who has taken a small child along on a series of errands can easily understand the effects of burnout on the Inner Artist. When the trip stretches a bit too long, children grow restless. More time passes and they get cranky. If the comfort of home isn't in sight soon, a complete and utter meltdown on the supermarket floor is likely to follow. Like other kids, our Artist doesn't have a huge attention span; even if we want to press on, we must respect her need for down time. (And now, I will do just that.)

Another case for working in moderation is our need for variety. Variety puts the sizzle in our creative lives and keeps our flow of ideas healthy and strong. When we first began our creative journey, we made conscious efforts to change our routines and try new things. Eventually, creating will be a very comfortable activity, and we can risk falling into a rut even when we're doing creative things. Even though we may be convinced that practicing for another hour will benefit us more than anything, often it's going out and taking a walk that will do us the most good. If we've been alone at our easel all day long, it might be time to shake things up by inviting our significant other to dinner and a movie. When we balance our favorite creative things with other healthy activities, we'll find that we return to our art forms with renewed energy and freshness.

FOR THE LOVE OF TREATS

Part of a healthy creative routine is being willing to treat ourselves once in a while. Contrary to popular belief, treating ourselves nicely can take quite a bit of discipline! How many times have we put a tasty box of blueberries or exciting carton of ice cream back on the supermarket shelf because we don't think we "need" it? This is appropriate behavior for people living in the grips of the scarcity mentality, but not for creators—we must be nice to ourselves, even if we have to train ourselves to do so. Leading lives of deprivation depletes our supply of ideas, but being willing to enrich our lives with small pleasures cultivates a healthy flow of inspiration. To learn the proper way to treat ourselves, we need only follow the example of the Creative Spirit, who sprinkles our lives with an abundance of miracles and opportunities. When we treat ourselves well, we make walking the creative path much more pleasurable and satisfying. By practicing taking good care of ourselves, we find that we can more easily reach the creative peaks we've always dreamed of.

Finishing

Numerous creative people sail through the early stages of the creative process, but have difficulty completing the final tasks: finishing the work, accepting it, and sending it out into the world. Many of us have completed ninety-five percent of the creative process many times, and we've ended up with drawers full of unpublished manuscripts and cabinets hiding beautiful yet unseen pottery—finished works that we assume aren't "good enough" to let anyone see. To realize our creative potential completely, we must learn how to take the leap of faith that is finishing.

Like many other pitfalls on the creative path, the holding in of our nearly finished projects is rooted in fear. Fear of finishing has much in common with fear of beginning. Worried about what others will think, what the reviews will sound like, and what changes our project might bring, we throw on the brakes, whether we're about to start or almost done. Because beginning fear and ending fear are so similar, it may help to return to Chapter Six and revisit our criticism-blasting techniques, or to take a trip back to Chapter Three and recall ways to face fear and uncertainty. However, the most powerful way I've found to finish and release creative works is by unleashing the power of the Creative Spirit.

As I mentioned earlier, finishing and releasing our projects is quite a leap of faith. When it's time to jump, having the Creative Spirit nearby can be a great source of strength and courage. Remember, the Spirit is a creator just like we are, a mighty friend who encourages us in our creative endeavors. The Spirit's support isn't around only when we feel happy and playful; rather, it's at its strongest when we're feeling weak and afraid. When we hit a hurdle of fear near the end of a creative project, a powerful way to calm ourselves is to call on the Creative Spirit. By saying a simple prayer like, "Please help me; I feel like I'm not good enough," we invite the Creative Spirit's Helping Hand to enter our lives in a profound and loving way. We don't even need to speak to receive this help; simply taking a few minutes to meditate or sit quietly with the Spirit can help drain the fear from our minds. The Spirit wants us to succeed; after all, it's usually the Spirit who inspired us to begin our projects in the first place! When we know there's a Helping Hand to catch us, there is no leap we need to fear.

> *It is good to have an end to journey toward, but it is the journey that matters in the end.*
>
> -Ursula K. Leguin

SUCCESS

If we walk far enough on our creative journey, nearly all of us will experience success. Our successes can be as simple as the rush we feel when we finish and release a project, or as grand as international fame and fortune. Either way, success is a culmination: of practicing our good habits, of being true to ourselves, of showing up at our work, of trusting our true capabilities. When we reach a peak of success, we owe it to ourselves and our Inner Artist to celebrate. Although we may have been told that it's selfish to toot our own horns, it's now time to put that untruth to rest. For creators, celebrating victories is an expression of gratitude. When we let out a big "WOOHOO!" over our finished work, we're saying "THANK YOU!" to the Creative Spirit. When we confidently share our work with other people, we come full-circle on our journey. We began by nurturing ourselves, and now, we are able to nurture others using our unique creative talents.

Using our creativity as a means to uplift and empower is the ultimate form of success. When we first picked up this book, many of us were fearful and uncertain about our creativity. We were the unfortunate recipients of negative messages that told us to ignore our creative desires. Now that we have taken this journey to uncover our creative talents, we can become bringers of the truth, bearers of the light. When we live joyful, healthy, and creative lives, we shine an intense beam of reality through the fog of society's myths. By continuing to nurture and protect our Inner Artist, we become a beacon of possibility to those who long to leave their hiding places behind. When we openly express ourselves and send our work out into the world, we illuminate others' lives with our unique understanding. As creators, we can bring radiance into a sometimes cloudy world.

A NEW BEGINNING

Achieving success is a priceless experience, but the true value of walking the creative path lies in continuing to learn and grow. Just as climbers can rest at the top of a mountain for only so long before they run out of food and water, we creators must limit the time we sit atop our successes. Exploration, not stagnation, is the way of creative living. "What's next?" is the Inner Artist's rallying cry. We maintain our creativity by continuing to broaden our horizons and expand our comfort zones. It is in this spirit of continued discovery that I close our time together with a call to begin anew. A call to celebrate our achievements while scanning the horizon for the next bright idea, the next wild opportunity, the next project that needs to be done. A call to continue on this rich and exhilarating journey that we call creativity.

WELCOME TO THE JOURNEY OF A LIFETIME!

Creative Homework

1. Let's Get Competent! - List some ways you can build your skills in each of Epstein's Four Core Competencies. Try to incorporate some of the activities you've listed into your daily life. Check out Dr. Epstein's quiz at http://www.mycreativityskills.com if you need help determining which of your competencies could use a boost.

2. Your Self-Discipline - Some of the landscapes we encounter on the creative journey require some self-discipline to cross. What does self-discipline mean to you? If negativity and lack are part of your current definition of self-discipline, how can you modify your understanding to make it more positive and empowering? What are some ways you will practice self-discipline as you continue your creative journey?

3 Finding your Space - This week, begin setting up a special place to create. If you can't practice your creative discipline in your home, begin devising a comforting ritual or pattern that brings creating into your daily routine. How will you decorate your space? What are some things you'd like to include in your creative routine? How can you continue to maintain a healthy creative practice even after you put this book back on the shelf?

4. What's in Your Sack? - Now that you're further along the creative path, open up your Sack O' Woe from Chapter One and take a look at your old worries and fears. Did any of them come true? If so, how did you react to them? Do any of them seem totally silly now that you look back at them?

5. Returning - As you venture to new destinations on your creative journey, always feel free to return to this book when you need guidance and strength!

References

Earley, Jay. (n.d.). *The people pleaser pattern: transforming compliance to autonomy*. Retrieved March 20, 2009 from http://www.earley.org/Patterns/people_pleaser.htm

Epstein, R. (1999). Generativity theory. In *Encyclopedia of Creativity*. (1999 ed., Vol. 1, pp. 759-766). San Diego: Academic Press.

Epstein, R. (2000). *The Big Book of Creativity Games: Quick, Fun Activities for Jumpstarting Innovation*. New York: McGraw-Hill.

Epstein, R. (2008). *Epstein Creativity Competencies Inventory for Individuals*. Retrieved March 23, 2009 from http://www.mycreativityskills.com

Fritz, R. (1991). *Creating*. New York: Fawcett.

Lewis, Jone Johnson. (2009). *Wisdom Quotes*. Retrieved March 19, 2009 from http://www.wisdomquotes.com

Messina, James J. (2009). *Overcoming Perfectionism*. Retrieved April 11, 2009 from http://www.livestrong.com/article/14702-overcoming-perfectionism

Osborn, A. (1957). *Applied Imagination: Principles and Procedures of Creative Thinking*. New York: Scribner.

Port, M. (2006). *Book Yourself Solid*. Hoboken, New Jersey: John Wiley and Sons.

Sills, J. (2008, November/December). Take this job and love it. *Psychology Today*, 41, 58-59.

Wallas, G. (1926). *The Art of Thought*. New York: Harcourt, Brace and Company.

On Becoming a WEC Guide

Newly-emerging creativity sprouts fragile and delicate buds, and these tiny beginnings must be nurtured in an equally graceful and caring way. If after reading this book, you are moved to use it to help others uncover and strengthen their creative abilities in a positive environment, I invite you to learn more about becoming an official *Women Embracing Creativity* Guide.

Guiding others toward achieving positive life changes can be quite challenging. Each person has her own unique learning style, starting point, and pace. Not everyone will understand things the same way we do, nor have the learning goals we think they should have. Balancing the varied aims and personalities of a group of savvy adult women can be difficult; however, maintaining this sense of balance, plus creating an unfaltering atmosphere of positivity and safety, are vital to successfully leading such a group along the creative path.

Held at Summerglen Music in Raleigh, North Carolina, WEC Guides' Training is designed to help you successfully navigate the challenges of leading the *Women Embracing Creativity* course. In your training, you'll learn how to guide from a tolerant place, keep the course simple yet powerful, and design activities to help strengthen participants' creative confidence. By completing our Guides' Training, you'll be granted exclusive rights to use the *Women Embracing Creativity* name, book, and *Guide's Guide* to lead courses and retreats of your own. For more information about WEC Guides' Training, please visit http://www.womenembracingcreativity.com/guides.

Index

2878747

Made in the USA